# DINDO GARCIA MAQUILING

# SUPERCHARGING PERSONAL EMPOWERMENT

*A STEP-BY-STEP WAY TO PERSONAL EMPOWERMENT*

Suite 300 - 990 Fort St
Victoria, BC, V8V 3K2
Canada

www.friesenpress.com

**Copyright © 2018 by Dindo Garcia Maquiling**
First Edition — 2018

All rights reserved.

No part of this publication may be reproduced in any form, or by any means, electronic or mechanical, including photocopying, recording, or any information browsing, storage, or retrieval system, without permission in writing from FriesenPress.

ISBN
978-1-5255-2359-5 (Hardcover)
978-1-5255-2360-1 (Paperback)
978-1-5255-2361-8 (eBook)

*1. RELIGION, CHRISTIAN LIFE, PROFESSIONAL GROWTH*

Distributed to the trade by The Ingram Book Company

# TABLE OF CONTENTS

| | |
|---|---|
| v | **Acknowledgements** |
| 1 | **Introduction** |
| 5 | **CHAPTER 1**<br>Understanding Me |
| 13 | **CHAPTER 2**<br>My Vulnerability |
| 21 | **CHAPTER 3**<br>Supercharging, Me? |
| 22 | A: Making Things Right |
| 25 | B: Manifesting Eagerness to Learn |
| 31 | C: Empowered by Encouragement |
| 35 | **CHAPTER 4**<br>Supercharging My Mind |
| 35 | A: Empowered through Endurance |
| 39 | B: Empowered through Persistence |
| 41 | C: Empowered through Patience |
| 44 | D: Empowered through Focus |
| 47 | **CHAPTER 5**<br>Supercharging the Body |
| 47 | A: Supercharging through Cleansing |
| 49 | B: Supercharging through Physical activity |
| 51 | C: Supercharged when Rested |
| 54 | D: Remember Karma |

| | |
|---|---|
| 57 | **CHAPTER 6** |
| | Supercharging the Spirit |
| 57 | A: Manifesting an Unwavering Faith |
| 61 | B: Manifesting a Blessed Hope |
| 66 | C: Manifesting High Motivation |
| 68 | D: Manifesting True, Lasting Happiness |
| 71 | **CHAPTER 7** |
| | Empowering my Social Life |
| 71 | A: Manifested through Fallen Walls |
| 73 | B: Manifested through Tolerance |
| 75 | C: Doing Daily Tasks – Manifesting Empowerment |
| 77 | D: Manifested through Asking the Right Questions |
| 81 | **CHAPTER 8** |
| | Supercharging My Economy |
| 81 | A: Manifesting Results |
| 84 | B: Manifested in Reaching Goals |
| 86 | C: Positivity Manifested |
| 90 | D: Manifesting Truth |
| 93 | **CHAPTER 9** |
| | Prescribing Solutions! |
| 93 | A: Manifesting Inward Change |
| 95 | B: Manifesting Power of Action |
| 97 | C: Manifesting Outward Change |
| 99 | D: Manifested through Abandoning the Old |
| 103 | **Conclusion** |
| 107 | **Appendix** |
| 113 | **Dindo Garcia Maquiling** |

# ACKNOWLEDGEMENTS

All glory and thanksgiving be given back to the Almighty Father, through His anointed and Appointed Son, **Dr. Apollo C. Quiboloy,** for the grace and mercy He continuously bestowed upon us. Thank you to all the prayers. Together with all Kingdom Administrators Sisters **Ingrid C. Canada, Teresita Dandan, Mariteo C. Canada, Nelida Lisada, Rosemarie N. Dimagnaong, Norie Cardona, Helen Panilag, Marlon Acobo, Marlon Rosete, Liza** and **Tata Amba**. Thank you for your prayers.

To my son **Dustin Nikko P. Maquiling**, who has supported his sister all the way until this very present moment, To **Lyn Nguyen**, who has been a friend forever; the regional director of Teavana, **Tammy Foss**, for her generous gifts to my daughter and for introducing us to the Gerson way; **Dr. Melvin Donato** our Gerson Therapy coach who patiently endeavour to guide and did a close monitoring and evaluation, who never gets tired to prepare adjustments to the protocol. Thanks to **Dr. Leonid Vinnitsky** who have been very patient in assisting us with various medical requests.

**To** my sister **Ruth Maquiling Hansen**, who immediately made the way for me to fly back to Vancouver Canada at the time my daughter, needed me the most. To **Lisa M. Parungao, my generous sister-in-law, my wife, Jocelyn P. Maquiling, my son Judah Meir and daughter Ruthie Gem,** who prayed earnestly and **Hiyasmin Panganiban**, the mother of both **Hannah Charis** and **Dustin Nikko** came to Canada to be with us during those difficult moments. To my mother, **Andrea G. Larsson**, was also assisting her husband, who at the same time was suffering from colon cancer, prayed for us and sent endless encouragement; to the rest of my siblings, **Nerisa, Ferdinand Maquiling and family, Myradel and family, Ruth Hansen and Family, Joshua Maquiling and family, David Maquiling and family**, all my relatives.

To all our friends, **Florita Bell** of England, **Priscilla Abayon** of Surrey BC, **Ana Makiling** of Aldergrove, **Tommy Uy** of Fleetwood, **Bernard and Marilou Locquiao** of Surrey BC, who cared enough to take me to the US border to get supplies; and all of those who have prayed for us during those years of our fiery test of faith. **To the entire Kingdom nation** who have regularly prayed for the healing of my daughter. You are the reason that we were so highly motivated to keep on, move on, lean on, and carry on.

## THANK YOU SO MUCH!

I am also grateful to all the staff of Friesen Press, **Mohammad Ghouri, Joshua Robinson, James Stewart, Miko Heddle,** who tirelessly coached me on how to get this book to its final stage, and to my editor, who encouraged me in making this book a reality.

And most of all to my daughter Hannah Charis, whose life inspired me to write this book, thank you.

She was born September 20, 1990, Hannah, HAPPY BIRTHDAY!!!

In 2017, after her recovery, this picture was taken in Sweden part of her 90 days European Tour on Board Yacht of her Aunt Ruth and Uncle Bent Hansen.

# INTRODUCTION

One of the most beautiful seasons in North America had just started. Yellow and orange leaves had begun to fall. The side streets filled with leaves, blown by a cool breeze. It was October 14, 2014, I had to rush my twenty-four-year-old daughter to the hospital. She was experiencing such severe chest pain that she could hardly breathe. She had been diagnosed with pneumonia by her family doctor a few months prior, and it had been recurring for several months, with symptoms I suspected were those of something else.

On that same day, I had to rush to the airport to fly to Hong Kong. I was caught in a situation where I had to decide whether to go ahead and fly or stay with my daughter in the hospital. It was a hard decision for me to make; I was torn between the two choices. I decided to leave her with her younger brother in the emergency room of Surrey Memorial Hospital while I traveled to Hong Kong. It was not an easy decision, considering that it's only myself and my children in Canada, with all our relatives in the Philippines.

While at the airport, I kept following up, checking how she was feeling. She was given oxygen to support her breathing, and the doctors ordered blood tests and other related vital physical examinations. All this occurred while I was at the airport, getting my boarding pass and boarding the plane later that night. I knew little about whatever it was that she was going through, and deep down in my heart, I was just praying that everything would be all right.

A lot of times in life, we do not understand the meaning behind the circumstances that greet us, yet we face them. I was not even sure what I would do if the results of her physical, blood, x-ray, and CT scan examinations were unfavorable, worse than I expected. There was fear deep within me regarding the outcome of her tests. I honestly didn't know if I could handle the situation; there was a lot of anxiety and worry, mingled with hope that whatever it was would be surmountable.

You might be facing similar situations in life today and can relate to what I am saying. Whatever you are facing, remember, dear, it is not the end of everything. Whatever circumstances you are experiencing right now, there is always hope. The meaning behind every challenge in life lies in the wisdom and understanding for which we gain from it. Do not allow discouragement to keep you from moving on.

Life presents us with numerous surprises, and what these might be often worries us. We are in constant anticipation of events that might occur, and we are not in control. None of us likes surprises in life; we like to know what is ahead of us, and we want to make sure that nothing will harm us. We try to figure everything out, only to be disappointed that we truly are not in control; someone up there controls us. He knows our tomorrow, and He knows every detail of our lives. He knows our weaknesses and our strengths. God doesn't give us anything that we're not strong enough to deal with, although a lot of times we think we are not strong enough. This book is written with you, the reader on mind, as you flip through the pages and navigate with me. Together, we explore. As Sylvester Stallone once said, **"As long as you are still alive your story is not over. Keep up the fight. Keep your dreams and hope alive. Go get it."**

There is hope even in a hopeless situation. Join me as we open the door to greater understanding and enlightenment. I am excited to walk with you every step of the way. Together, we will learn the paths that lead us to greater heights of faith, where we will see every possibility manifested on our way, regardless of how challenging our circumstances may be.

# CHAPTER 1

## UNDERSTANDING ME

If there is one person that we need to know, it is ourselves. We should know who we are, what weakens us, what makes us vulnerable, what strengths we possess, and most of all, what inner qualities we have that allow us to overcome life's challenges. Knowing our weaknesses allows us to see the things in life that stop us from doing what is right. What hinders us from accomplishing what needs to be done? Awareness of our weaknesses will allow us to be cautious, to not allow those things to dominate our consciousness, and to overcome them. I remember Martin Luther said,

> **"You** cannot keep birds from flying over your head but you can keep them from building a nest in your hair"

We cannot allow our circumstances to overwhelm us, when we focus on things that increase anxiety, double our fear, magnify our weaknesses, and destroy the citadel of faith. When we begin to falter, we are shown the reality of our strength; our response is a manifestation of who we really are. We cannot hide the fact that a lot of times we succumb more than we overcome. That is our reality.

When we understand the power of our strength, we consider the positive side of things, exploring every window of possibility. There are inner qualities of greatness inside us, which need to be enhanced and brought to the surface. When we allow our strength, we will overcome every challenge that comes our way. When we know our strengths and weaknesses, we can easily identify the symptoms that drag us down, identify those things that reduce us to the point that our challenges become bigger than our faith. Once we have done that, we can begin to walk the path by which the impossible becomes possible.

While I was on that Boeing 777 bound for Hong Kong, deep inside me were puzzling questions. I felt so alone thinking about my daughter, 37,000 km below me. Would she be able to survive this ordeal? What if something happened to her? Seated at the far back of the plane, I had mixed emotions. I took a deep breath, and the guy in front of me smiled. I smiled in return and introduced myself. We chatted a little bit, and I mentioned how ended up at the rear, when I asked the crew to put me near the front. He laughed looking at my angry face.

That was the beginning of our long conversation. We exchanged questions about where we were in the Philippines, a very typical Filipino question. He mentioned that he was not from Vancouver, just visiting someone, and that he was just passing through. We talked about a lot of things, and he began asking me about my spiritual journey, mentioning that he too was on a spiritual journey.

I couldn't concentrate while we were talking, for my mind was in the middle of something, right? When our mind is occupied with worries, it's hard to communicate because our hearing becomes dull; we listen to people's comments as if they are all against us. We become very defensive, covering up a sense of inferiority or hiding our sense of inadequacy. It is understandable. To be frail is human, as they say. You are not alone; we all go through those moments when we are mentally blocked.

I replied, "Yes I was in a spiritual journey "and I've found what I've been looking for."

He asked me, "Where and how did you find it?"

I told him, "Let me share my response with you in a moment."

He was adamant about knowing what I had to say next, but the flight stewards began their rounds, providing hot meals. We stopped and enjoyed our sumptuous meal that night.

I remember my mother, who had a great influence on the way I respond to challenges; she went through many things in life too. I could devote a whole book to her life story. This is what she had to say: "You deplete your energy when you do not have the right focus. Whatever your eyes are focusing on, that will determine your vision, will determine what your perspective in life will be." It makes sense, right? What are we gazing at? Do we focus on our minuscule circumstances and forget to consider the gargantuan power of the Almighty? This is our failure. We tend to focus on the wrong thing, which has poor results.

Human tendency is to blame ourselves. We put all the blame on ourselves and end up committing suicide, or we put all the blame on other people and wash our hands of any guilt. We cannot live a life of blame. If we make mistakes, let's make amends, seek reconciliation, and straighten our path. And let's forgive those who have, one way or another, contributed to the pain we are going through. I will discuss this topic further in a separate chapter.

I like to read books that help me refocus my thoughts, realign my thinking. Our mind is very powerful. It can create things, whether good or bad. It depends on what we are preoccupied with. Crucial to our empowerment are the things that occupy our mind. We must be on guard for things that pollute our thinking and take away wisdom. I remember a verse in scripture that says, "If there be any virtue, if there be any praise, think on these things" (Philippians 4:8 KJV). Yes, but what are these things? "Whatsoever things are true, whatsoever things are honest, whatsoever things are just, whatsoever things are pure, whatsoever things are lovely, whatsoever things are of good report; if there be any virtue, and if there be any praise, *think on these things*" (Philippians 4:8 KJV, emphasis added). Allow me to add one more quotation, from a man full of wisdom, King Solomon: "For what a man thinketh in his heart, so is he" (Proverbs 23:7 KJV). We are what we think; we become that with which we are preoccupied.

In the Holy Scriptures, King David wrote, **"For I am fearfully and wonderfully made"** (Psalms 139:14 KJV). The understanding of our beginning provides the path back to our Creator, the master designer of all creation, as King David put in words: "The heavens declare the glory of God; and the firmament showeth his handiwork (Psalms 19:1 KJV). The apostle Paul added to this, saying, "For we are his workmanship, created in Christ Jesus" (Ephesians 2:10 KJV). We are a masterpiece of the omnipotent, omniscient, omnipresent Creator of the heavens and the earth. He designed the universe; He had a master plan for my very life, so unique that it's only me who can make it happen.

He created us in His image; He gave us our mind, our emotions, and our will, and this is the image of God in us. He created us to have a covenant relationship with him, a covenant relationship by which we become His son, by which He, the unseen God, will come inside of us and reside and walk on earth through us. This is our origin; for this reason, we are here. And our in-depth understanding of this matter will determine the kind of life we are living, the destiny toward which we are heading.

I asked my newfound friend on the plane what he did for a living.

He replied, "I'm a doctor from the Bahamas, been working there for many years."

What a coincidence, right? I asked him, "In what field?"

He replied, "A medical doctor."

So, I asked him, "Can I share my daughter's health issues?"

"Sure," he said.

I began sharing, "She has had an off-and-on dry cough for many months. Doctors ruled out pneumonia. She's at the emergency department of the hospital as we speak."

Then he asked me, "Does cancer run in your family or her mother's?"

"Not that I know of."

He took a paper and a pen and scribbled down the names of the three different blood examinations, explaining, "Doctors won't order any of these blood exams unless worse symptoms are coming up. Asked your daughter to request that her doctor do these blood exams as soon as possible." Then he sighed and said, "I hope they will."

Up in the skies, I texted my daughter, who replied, "I got it, Dad." I texted her back to really insist her doctor order these blood exams. I wondered how my text message had reached her, then after a while, I received a phone call from a friend in Vancouver. I was puzzled by how her call had reached me.

The doctor just smiled and asked me, "You texted her and she got it, right? Nice."

I expressed my gratitude for the time we had spent sharing that night, then we unwound a bit and enjoyed the duration of the thirteen-hour flight to Hong Kong.

Contemplating the doctor's question about whether I had cancer in my family, I felt a deep feeling of fear. What if? And if it is, can I handle the situation? What shall I do? I kept asking myself. "There is nothing you can do," said a still small voice inside of me.

So many times, in the past, I have gone through experiences that I believe contribute to and pile up through these years. I know my strengths and weaknesses; I understand where I am most vulnerable. This gives me the understanding that nothing happens in the life of a person that God will not allow.

A lot of times we ask, "Why do bad things happen to good people?" And I would say, "Why not? Are bad people the only ones who deserve to be tested?" All of us, I believe—even myself—deserve to be tested so that we know our strength, so we know where we are most weak, and so we know where we are stronger. I like examinations and evaluations because through them I will determine my highest and lowest score, where I need to improve myself, and where I excel. Knowing these things, in turn, will allow you to make a step-by-step plan for improving your lowest score and working on areas where you are weak. It is very important that we do not remain stagnant in areas that will benefit us. Every day should be a step upward, going higher and higher until we reach success.

The months during which my daughter, Hannah, and I worked together to make the Gerson therapy works, were a time of adjustment, of teaching each other. The more I loved my daughter, the more sympathetic I was to her. We learned to chat for hours and talked about life, about death, and about life after this life. There is a strong inner bond that holds us together in times of difficulty. We learned to hold hands and move on, no matter what it took to live. Life is borrowed, a gift that can be extended or taken by the giver. We must enjoy it. If you haven't told your parents "I love you" or "Please forgive me," please do it while they can still hear you, while you can still mend the broken relationship.

Bitterness will only produce more hatred, grievances, and fear. Why not stop for a moment and go to the person you have wronged, no matter how small or how big the wrong, and ask for forgiveness. It will open the way to freedom. You will have an inner release. You'd better let it go, and let God be in control.

I was away from my children for four years, separated. My absence carved negative memories in my children, especially Hannah. She had been so close to me since she was little. I remember one time that I was sick in bed; she came to me and said, "Dad, you need medicine? You want me to pray for you?" Hannah was five years old at that time, May of 1995.

Recalling those moments while she was lying in bed grieves my heart. During those critical moments, looking at my daughter, I didn't know whether she would live or die. Deep within me I cried, asking for help: "Lord, heal my daughter, give her another chance to live." My innermost being sobbed, begging God, "Please answer my prayer." I felt that I must be strong for her, that I could not allow her to see me crying. But there is nothing wrong with crying; it keeps from becoming heartbroken.

As we continue to the next chapter, let's remember that being aware of where you are most vulnerable will give you the chance to overcome those vulnerabilities.

# CHAPTER 2

## MY VULNERABILITY

We learned nursery rhymes when we were kids. "Humpty Dumpty" rang in our ears. When he had a great fall, it was when he sat on the wall, making himself vulnerable. He broke into pieces, and all the king's horsemen couldn't put Humpty Dumpty together again. I mentioned in the last chapter, we must understand who we are, so that we won't allow ourselves into a situation like Humpty Dumpty, sitting where he was most vulnerable: on the wall. Get away from the edge of the cliff. Even when a notice says, "Don't touch, it's wet," we touch it anyway, or when the high voltage notice that says, "Do not touch high voltage" still explode ourselves anyway.

Knowing ourselves includes understanding our strength and weakness. Allow me to explain further why we become vulnerable. First and foremost, within us lives a person who hasn't grown up. Our minds are part and parcel of the culture we came from, the education we received from home and school, and the sermons we heard from the pulpit. These were the mental food we grew up with and which became our value system, which we've carried all these years. Our thought patterns are a by-product of what we learned from these schools of thought. This forms our convictions and belief system, which are by-products of our formal and non-formal education.

Second, our emotions are dominated by our thoughts. We feel what our mind makes us feel; we might become depressed and gloomy, depriving us of enjoying what life has to offer. When, in times of hardship, we are emotionally disturbed, experiencing discouragement, it means we are weak and not strong. Hardships are not intended to diminish our power to think and make the right decisions. Within us is a weak mind that can become the Devil's playground. We can become weak in our emotions. We can easily give up on life, give up enjoying every moment, during challenging experiences.

Third, our will is also influenced by our mind; it makes decisions according to what the mind dictates to be right and wrong. When fear fills our hearts, when we fear what the future holds, trying to figure things out and speculate, we do not know what to do. We become helpless, puzzled, and depressed. We must have a strong will, capable of making the right decisions.

Fourth, our body reacts to our thoughts and feelings, and we make decisions and begin to increase acidity by worrying. This acidity builds up and results in hormonal imbalances, which produce inflammation in the gut, then rashes and unexplained skin irritations. When you will become restless, sleeping fewer hours, you will experience decreased of mobility you might then end up experiencing serious illnesses.

Fifth, since our minds are filled with doubt, we begin questioning the Creator, asking, "Why have you created me? Why am I here?" Our questioning of the Creator—you know why it happens—occurs because we do not know who we really are. We become unstable in all ways.

Most of all, sixth, we lack faith. When you lose faith, all you have are worries, fears, resentment, blame, doubts, paranoia, sickness will follow. You begin to ask question who God is, and ask if God does really exist? Faithlessness produces failure, unproductivity, decrease of energy, emptiness, blurs perspective and brings death.

Furthermore, there are physical manifestations, that accompany disempowerment, which are the following:

First is *lack of sleep*. When we are not properly rested, the whole system of the body is affected. Sleep at least eight hours a day. Rest between three to four hours of work; have an awesome break. Our mind can only think so much at a time; it must find some refreshing moments.

Second, *the food that we eat* and liquids that we drink affect the way we carry ourselves; some challenges need physical strength. Good, regular walking exercise could be the best way to inhale fresh air and exhale the bad air inside of us. Eat and drink alkaline.

Third, when we are *overly exhausted*, this affects the way we think, and affects our ability to make the right decision at a given time. As much as possible, prevent overload; as humans, we can only do so much at any given time and, of course, depending on our capacity.

The fourth is never put your body at *risk of breaking down*. There is the person who expires in the middle of their work, there are those few who will not wake up the following morning. There will be a day of reckoning. We will pay a toll for all the things we have done to our body. We should take this precious moment to live and treasure the memories we create.

Our vulnerability will be tested! Are we ready to take the test? Are we mentally, emotionally, physically, financially, and spiritually ready for a hard blow? Our readiness is very important. We must be prepared before the time of battle.

After a month and a half, I received a call from my daughter saying she had cancer, Hodgkin's lymphoma, stage 3. Her naturopath's chest examination and the blood exams I asked her to do while I was on my flight confirmed she had cancer. I was shocked and horrified by the feeling of my daughter's pain inside me. It was not easy. There was silence for a moment. Deep within me, I was crying, asking for help. I was terrified of what her illness might become. I was not sure how to go about dealing with a worse-case scenario. I was kind of lost for a moment.

I requested that my cousin, Dr. Rene Guinto to call the doctor that I met on the plane. Even today, during the writing of this book, I have never heard anything about him. I have sent numerous emails thanking him, but there has been no reply at all. Was he an angel? If he was not an angel, who was he? I feel like I was touched by an angel; the man I was talking to on that plane while I worried about my daughter was an angel, sent by God to assist me at a time when I needed Him the most.

God sends angels to assist us in difficult times in our lives. They come to rescue us, sometimes from impending death. I remember a November 28, 2016, CNN story about an eight-month-old baby girl who was ejected from a car after the car was swept away by a truck. Everyone looked on the ground nearby, hoping to find the baby. After hearing a sound, they found her inside a storm drain, two dozen feet from the crash site—unharmed. If angels are not real and ready to rescue people's lives, that baby could have been dead. One of the firefighters said, "There had to be divine intervention for her to end up being OK."

Yes, we will be tested to determine our limitations. When we react with faith, it opens different avenues of possibilities. Our response at this moment is crucial to what the universe will do, as it acts on our behalf. The law of attraction mentions that we attract the things we want to happen to us. It all depends upon us—upon our wishes, our desires. Flying back to Vancouver after a month, passing through South Korea, was the saddest trip I'd ever taken, coming home to my daughter in the hospital, lying there facing a horrible disease. I felt so sad, but I had strong faith, and believed that God would make a way. I said to myself, "God giveth and God taketh away." I strengthened my resolve that no matter what, I would trust Him with all my heart.

A few weeks after Hannah was diagnosed with cancer, the concert crusade of Pastor Apollo C. Quiboloy was coming up: January 25, 2015. My daughter and I planned to attend and will ask Pastor Apollo to pray and lay his hands on her. We went that night, and my daughter was touched by an angel, I suppose, right after his hands were laid upon her. While we had our dinner, she testified that she was touched not only by an angel, but also by God. She exclaimed, "I felt the compassionate love of God in his hands, and I saw the eyes of Jesus in his eyes." After that, healing began to take place in the unseen world.

I never doubted God, and I was never worried again. Words came to my mind: "Worrying is an insult to the omnipotent God." We can only believe and trust him, for He works in a miraculous way. Indeed, just at the thought of it, I gaze toward heaven and say, "Father Almighty, thank you, you are worthy of all praise. I worship you."

We can only be grateful every day there is no reason to complain. Our lips filled with praise, our voices lift to the heavens from whence our help comes. There is an innermost power that is created within us as we live a life in full obedience to His will. It is His will that we trust Him and honor him even in difficult times. When you're about to give up, He is there at the very end of the rope; at the end of your resources, He is always there.

When our batteries are low, He is our charging point; that's where our help comes from. The increase of energy come from the source; when we are connected, we can be fully charged. Sometimes we are permitted by God to experience being tossed toss by the winds of trial and hardship, so that we may know that He is God. When He comes to the rescue, He comes when we need Him the most—and He is never too late in his response.

Our vulnerability is an opportunity for us to see the almighty power of God at work in our lives. As He once said, **"My grace is sufficient for you, for my power is made perfect in weakness"** (2 Corinthians 12:9 NIV). Then Paul added, "...**when I am weak, then am I strong**" (2 Corinthians 12:10 KJV).

**2nd Corinthians 12:9**

When we become weak, He will give us grace that can sustain us through severe trials. This unmerited favor is enough to carry us through, nothing else. His power will come to the rescue—not power of our own making, but His orchestration in our lives. We are made complete through Him. Is this not a great comfort? This is what made my daughter and me strong and kept us going all those twenty-four months; the goodness of the Lord never fails. Meditate upon the words of the apostle Paul to the Galatian Church: **"But my God shall supply all your need according to his riches in glory by Christ Jesus"** (Philippians 4:19 KJV). We may be tempted to worry not at all, for the abundance of God's mercy is made available. He surely did supply our need, according to His riches.

God will never be too late in meeting our needs; He always comes on time. There are times we feel He is too late in replying, yet when we look at the clock He is just on time. Never doubt, God never turns His back on his promises; they will all come true. Let's move along as we discover ourselves in a deeper way, as we explore how we can supercharge ourselves.

# CHAPTER 3

## SUPERCHARGING, ME?

You've got to be kidding. Me, supercharging myself, with what? We sometimes panic about where to find a charging point, fearing that we might run out of power. We must find our way to reconnect to the source, to find our way back to fullness. We can supercharge ourselves, depending on the adaptor we are using. Whether an adaptor is for supercharging or a slow charge depends upon the charger and the cable we are using; an extra power charge is sometimes needed to shorten the waiting time.

There are moments in my life when I have felt totally lost, when I haven't known where I'm going, when I have had no direction at all. These were times when I lost touch with the meaning of existence; I felt such dryness within my soul that sometimes I didn't even like to pray anymore. I didn't have the passion I had before. I lost the first touch of God in my life, what was wrong with me during these difficult times? I hate this feeling. I feel it especially when I hear some bad news. It makes me ask why bad things happen to good people. Why my daughter, God? Are there not more bad people, people worse than us, people who deserve to be sick and die? My daughter is very young; she's only twenty-four years old, full of dreams and aspirations. Why, Lord? Questions spread like cobwebs through my mind. We might ask ourselves what we have done to make things right.

## A: *MAKING THINGS RIGHT*

This is a moment of asking deeper meaningful questions. What have I done that might have contributed to her sickness? Did I make a mistake that has contributed to her ailment? Should there be an evaluation of her medical records? Was there any food or any medications that triggered her cancer cells to be active?

In my mind, there was a need to make things right, after my daughter was diagnosed with cancer, her mother was immediately informed and booked a trip to come over to Vancouver and visit her. I found out later that my daughter's mother's aunt had died with cancer, cancer runs in the bloodline of her mother. Deep within my soul, there was peace, knowing that God is in control.

Eight months prior, my daughter had been so stressed out with her job at Teavana; she was the senior manager, supervising the stores at Metrotown and Guildford malls. During this time, she was being groomed to be a regional manager for Teavana's chain of stores. She took her job seriously; we thought it would be the culprit in all of this.

We were also wondering if, because she was exposure to many different varieties of tea, some might have been contaminated or exposed her to some form of radiation, especially the matcha green tea from Japan. Yes, we were considering every possible cause for her sickness. Making things right, I suppose, with whatever we could come up with—only God knows the reasons for and purpose of this happening to her and to us as a family.

Do we know the purpose? Maybe not while we are in the middle of the challenge. Did we have a clear understanding of what was going on and what the climax of this story would be? We were without a clue! We could hope for the best, but everything depends upon God. We exist not by chance; rather, we are God's creation of His own hands. We are His masterpiece.

Our minds are sharp enough to analyze and understand reasons for human suffering. We rationalize the facts available to us, or maybe on some clinical studies, to answer the millions of questions from our finite minds. These inquisitive minds seek answers to an unending list of questions, leading us to speculate, calculate facts, and find theories that might satisfy our quest for answers.

We are not ready when unexpected events happen in our lives; the surprises come, and all our dreams are torn apart. The human tendency is to be upset, to be afraid of what the future holds. Our outlook becomes so bleak; our faith staggers and we can no longer see the beautiful story unfolding through our pain and agony. These feelings are as real as you and me. We face fiery trials, we feel the heat that is bombarding our comfort zone, and that makes us afraid to move forward.

We cannot hide ourselves in denial; we must face these trials with courage. While we are in this physical state, we feel this entire negative vibe; it takes time to understand the reasons. Our gratefulness in any situation will be rewarded either here in this present life or in the life hereafter. The apostle Paul mentioned this in one of his letters to the Galatian Church, saying, "In everything give thanks: for this is the will of God" (1 Thessalonians 5:18 KJV). Is it God's will for us to be sick? Why not? If He is putting us to the test, it is to develop our character and strong faith.

**in everything gives thanks**

Our role is to mend our ways, increasing awareness and sensibility to eternal values. We look back and read the ancient book, which leads us to the perfect way. It may not be as simple as we think it is, but it pays to heed the call of the Creator, which says, "Harden not your hearts, as in the provocation" (Hebrews 3: 15 KJV). We will be put to severe tests, and the real issues that cause us to falter will surface through those tests. The real you will come out when tried and tested. Our adherence to His call will lead us to eternal bliss or eternal suffering. When you are being tested, soften your heart; do not be callous when God is testing you.

Making things right, following the path to inner healing, begins with our thoughts, which will either block the way to healing or open the way to enlightenment. We must open ourselves to the Lord of all spirits, allowing Him to open the doors to overflowing knowledge and understanding. Understand the human body and the healing God has provided to all humanity. Understanding "the beautiful truth" make us to believe that indeed the Almighty Creator truly understands human anatomy and has provided everything in the Garden for healing, wellness, and happiness. Let us go back to the state of wholeness which we will live in the Garden of Eden again.

While thirty thousand feet above the ground, on board United Airlines Flight 809 on August 16, 2017, from San Francisco, California, bound for Hong Kong, these thoughts came into my mind: "Doing things God's way requires continuous evaluation. We must learn to make things excellent by practising doing right at the very start, but our eagerness to learn from Him is a prerequisite."

## *B:* MANIFESTING EAGERNESS TO LEARN

Learning is a process that each person must do intentionally; it's hard to teach when readiness to learn does not exist. Learning, whether through formal education or lessons learned from life experiences, has no end; it is part of who we are and what we become through time.

We learn from the decisions we make every day, whether they are good or bad; the lessons of failures and successes are enormous. We cannot ignore the lessons of failure; they allow us to evaluate what we did wrong and reposition ourselves for success. There must always be a readiness to learn in every aspect of our lives—the value of it is more than taking a course at Harvard University. There are lessons that can't be learned in the higher establishments of learning. A lot is learned in the mundane things that we do daily; bits and pieces of life provide us valuable lessons that can make us or break us.

The decision my daughter would be making was between life and death. I remember the words that she said, after the second session of chemotherapy: "Dad, if I die, I'd rather die without any pain. Chemotherapy is more painful than any pain induced by my cancer." It was not an easy decision to make, but we had to decide anyway. We decided to put the rest of the twelve sessions her oncologist prescribed on hold. It was a tug of war. As William Shakespeare stated, "To be, or not to be: that is the question:/Whether 'tis nobler in the mind to suffer/ The slings and arrows of outrageous fortune, / Or to take arms against a sea of troubles, / And by opposing end them?" (*Hamlet* 3.2.57–61).

Learning to *trust*—it wasn't easy to trust the advice of doctors who practice modern medicine. But we were taught that whatever our doctor says is the truth. The chemotherapy, chemically diffused inside the vein, targets the cancer cells, but at the same time destroys the rest of the body. The Gerson way on the other hand, is to "heal the body and the body will heal itself," and get rid of its own diseases. Most medical practitioners know what pharmaceutical drugs they can prescribe to their patients; instead of helping them find health, patients became dependent all their lives on their medication.

Learning to *obey* is not so easy. I had a struggle with my daughter's oncologist, who wanted us to follow his pharmaceutical-inclined protocol. He did not offer us any other options or any alternative solutions to chemotherapy or radiation. He was so adamant that my daughter goes through the twelve chemo sessions. During this moment of struggle, we were introduced to the work of Dr. Max Gerson, the very controversial doctor who claimed to have found the cure for cancer and debated his way into the American Senate in the early forties and during the Second World War. He published is clinical research, with at least five hundred success stories. He was denied acceptance, by the mainstream medical establishment he loses the case, which favored the pharmaceutical companies. My daughter and I trusted our instincts and followed the path of Gerson therapy.

There are many lessons to learn in life. One of them is *faith*: believing something will happen even if it seems impossible. When we look at our reality, we are limited to our own resources; faith allows us to see beyond what we have and to consider the horizon of the infinite. Miracles can happen. We read about them in every recorded history—stories of the lives of people who have gone through various experiences, which show us that indeed supernatural interventions are still happening in the world today. You just must believe it, and the universe will make it happen.

While some people consider the emptiness of life, positivism considers every possibility rather than the difficulty. We need to see the brighter picture even during dark times; a positive thinker will see beautiful flowers blooming in their mind as they close their eyes. This mind does not settle on what cannot be done but zeroes in what can be done in very adverse circumstances. Never be discouraged. Take a poll of every option, every solution, and every way and means to make things happen. People with positive mindset are problem-solvers, solution-seekers, and results-oriented people. That is exactly what we did when we got hold of Charlotte and Dr. Max Gerson's book. We found an alternative way that might promote the possibility of healing the body and eventually get rid of any diseases, including cancer.

We also watched *The Beautiful Truth* (2008), a documentary film made by a student completing his homeschool course work and at the same time finding the answers to his mother's earlier death from cancer (vitamin B17 deficiency).

We can learn to grow by supercharging ourselves. It is expected that growth happens naturally. Corn has different stages of growth; when we bury the seed under the soil, the seed itself doesn't die, it begins to grow, and a new life emerges, bearing the features of the seed. The new shoot grows to the surface of the soil, followed by the stem, which gets stronger over time, then leaves. The stalks begin to grow taller and taller, and then the flowers begin to bloom. The corncob begins to emerge, soft and tender, and eventually seeds begins to appear. When harvest time comes—either when the cob is young and ready to eat or mature and ready to be replanted for more crops or preservation, stored for the next season. Yes, growth is an expectation of every farmer; we expect progress. No matter what happens, growth is sought after.

When a tree is grown up, it bears the fruits of its kind, and every fruit is pleasing to the eye, admired and desired. Many fruits can aid healing during illnesses and could save thousands of lives. Every day in her protocol included thirteen (13) glasses of eight ounces from organic-certified fruit and vegetable juices, with twenty-four different supplements to augment the vitamins and minerals in her body, depleted due to two sessions of chemotherapy.

In going back to the Gerson therapy, we did some research and listened to testimonials from people who had gone through similar therapy. We finally decided to go for the full Gerson therapy protocol. Dr. Melvin Donato was very accommodating in assisting us with our decision. It wasn't easy, and we started with no knowledge at all, but we followed the path. Little by little, as we went through the process, we learned so much. We both became learners, being taught the Gerson way step by step. During these times, I attended personally to my daughter's needs. I stopped working and became her primary caregiver.

This beautiful earth was created by God to be able to sustain itself. Every plant in His creation has the capacity to bring health and healing to our bodies; we must grow in this knowledge and understanding. We are not guinea pigs in the hands of researchers and scientists, to be tested and tried with their so-called advanced medicine, right?

Please read Charlotte Gerson's book, *The Gerson Therapy – Revised and Updated: The Proven Nutritional Program for Cancer and Other Illnesses*, October 1, 2001, Charlotte Gerson, founder of the Gerson Institute, is the daughter of Dr. Max Gerson. Under her father's tutelage, Charlotte learned about the remarkable nutritional therapy that has saved the health of thousands, including Nobel Peace Prize winner Dr. Albert Schweitzer, a life-long advocate of the Gerson therapy. Charlotte has supervised the training of medical staff at the Gerson Institute and at hospitals licensed to teach the Gerson Institute's method.

Learning our way back to Him will have a big difference in the way we live; our lifestyle will be enhanced by the spiritual understanding we develop about our temporary existence on the planet. Values will be well-engraved, with a deeper commitment to lasting peace, joy, love, and camaraderie. We have an inner longing for community, cooperation, and collaboration, rather than factions and divisions. It is to our advantage that we be attuned to our Maker; coherence and unified spiritualism produces healing that is both physical and spiritual.

A deep sense of understanding of why diseases, pain, and suffering come into our lives. We don't know when our end will be. When my daughter's oncologist demanded that she go back to the third chemotherapy session and finish off the twelve sessions he'd prescribed, he looked at me with fiery eyes, saying, "Don't you know, Mr. Maquiling, that if your daughter won't go on with the next ten sessions, she will die in one to three months? If she continues, she could live another year or more."

I became furious and replied, "Who are you, sentencing my daughter to death? Are you God?" I then asked him, "Doctor, do you have children?"

He replied, "Yes, I do."

"How old are they?"

He said, "One is six years old and the other one is eight years old."

"Very well. What if I tell you one of them is dying in three months? How will you feel? How will you take it? You and I could die today, right, doctor? Who are we to schedule a person's death sentence?" He went out of the room and left me, my daughter, and her mother.

We must learn to commune in our inner being, that still, small voice that tells us whether we are headed in the right direction or not. Contemplating the goodness of God made me feel that He was with me, even at this most trying of moments. He is ready to guide me, teaching me the right path. You might be confused, not knowing what to do when confronted with various options. The God who lives in you will show you the way.

**"Our surmountable challenges are not comparable to the gargantuan power of the Almighty."**

As I write this chapter, I am in Macao, China; looking at thousands of people running towards the casinos grieves my soul. I cannot imagine how blind people can be, how they can be ignorant of the divine plan. They aim to win the game even when what is at stake is their wealth and fame. They never learn to know what the Creator has for them; they have wasted their lives, wasted their time, living their lives as if there is no end.

I learned to take an account of my own personal life as I considered the lives of these people from different parts of the globe, people who had come to the Las Vegas of Asia to find luck by gambling their lives. We cannot gamble our lives, expecting to win, when we already knew we are on the losing side. Chemotherapy is a gamble that medical doctors, pharmaceutical companies, and all their advocates want us to play.

In Canada, chemotherapy is free. You don't have to pay anything. You must make yourself available, sign the waiver, and you are off to go on the painful ride of chemotherapy. Please watch for my next book for very detailed facts and the results of my daughter's battle with cancer.

## C: EMPOWERED BY ENCOURAGEMENT

When you fail many times, using different methods and plans, keep going; maybe the next time will bring success and happiness. Our great inventors were given by God the minds to be able to grasp different formulas, and given knowledge, understanding, and wisdom during difficult time. They looked at things differently and saw ahead, contributing to a human history of success in technology. They laid the foundation for future inventors to accomplish works greater than their own, advancing, improving, creating, and innovating their masterpieces, giving people a better way of life and doing excellent things.

Trial and error contributes towards great success, whether inventing light bulbs, telephones, computers, telecommunications, or farm machines. These great inventors never give up. When Sir Thomas Edison have done hundred trials with his invention of the incandescent light, this is what he had to say: "Failures are stepping stones towards success." Success comes through many failures, because when we rise when we fail, when we move on when we fail, we will succeed, if we won't give up. Confucius had these words to say: "Our greatest glory is not in never falling but in rising every time we fall." Yes, we rise every time we fall, for failure is not the end, it is the beginning of a new dawn, a new triumphant story to share. Robert Kennedy put it this way: "Only those who dare to fail greatly can achieve greatly." Failure has taught us valuable lessons.

> **"Every great cause is born from repeated failures and from imperfect achievements."**
>
> —Maria Montessori

We are motivated not to make lots of mistakes; rather, we are taught that even when we have done the best we could make things right, we still fail. Just keep going. Never give up until you reach your dream. This is what the sports legend Michael Jordan has to say: "I've missed more than nine thousand shots in my career. I've lost almost three hundred games. Twenty-six times, I've been trusted to take the game-winning shot…and missed. I've failed over and repeatedly in my life. That is why I succeed."

Beautiful words of wisdom; no matter what happens, we keep going. Soon, we'll see the door of opportunity open wide in front of us, making the work of our hands perfect.

Look at our two hands, which can do wonders, can create and make magnificent works of art, make miracles, hands that can touch one solitary soul. Hands that stop the winds from blowing, hands that made five loaves and two fishes feed five thousand hungry people. The pair of hands crucified on the cross are the same hands that open to invite us all to "Come and I will give you rest." Hands that heal the sick, make the blind see, and the hunchback straight.

# CHAPTER 4

## SUPERCHARGING MY MIND

### A: EMPOWERED THROUGH ENDURANCE

We all go through hardships in life; this is part of our human existence. No one is exempted; everyone will go through trials, which will vary in size and come in different forms the intensity and magnitude unique to every individual. Challenges come in so many beautiful shapes, mostly designed according to our own strength and capacity. Your load of trials depends on your power to endure; you may tear a little, you may bleed sometimes. But when you're determined and look at every circumstance as part of the growing process, healing has begun.

During the early days of my daughter's Gerson protocol, we meticulously followed each measurement—the number of glutathione drops per eight ounces of juice, which drops came first and what was next. It must be precise to achieve the best results. I washed all the organic fruit, green apples, carrots, lettuce, green peppers, and much more. There were times that we ran out of organic carrots, or Granny Smith apples. This protocol needs a strong, determined mind willing to endure and attend to the very least detail, with consistency and close monitoring and timing; otherwise, you won't get the best results.

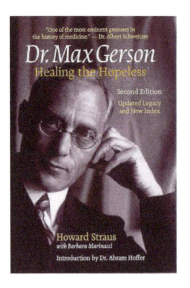 

For more information, please get a copy of this valuable book and read it; it's worth of your investment whether you have cancer or not. Please visit this website and purchase these books.

http://store.gerson.org/Books/?_ ga=2.246019588.1811112514.1516906714-960862959.1516906714

The writings of Apostle Paul, who went thru severe trials and persecution, were jailed for no reason other than being passionate about his mission. He was a man who, regardless how bad the things were that he went through, remained resilient, allowing time to change the status quo. Jailed for many years in a Roman cell prior to his execution by beheading, he wrote,

> *There hath no temptation taken you, but such as is common to man: but God is faithful, who will not suffer you to be tempted above that ye are able; but wherewith the temptation also makes a way to escape, that ye may be able to bear it. (1 Corinthians 10:13 KJV)*

The truth is, hardships are given according to our ability to endure. Trials are designed to make us better and not bitter, and empathetic to people who are going through similar experiences. It is very encouraging to know that "God is faithful." He is there with you through the process of pain, and He is there when you are almost at the point of giving up. There were numerous times my daughter was in pain and she would tell me, "Dad, I can't do it anymore. The pain is beyond what I can bear. I'm giving up."

As her primary caregiver, I had to be strong. I reminded her of God's word, which says, "I will never leave you nor forsake you," especially now, in a time of severe pain, when you need Him the most. I tried to give her words that would give her life, hope, and love.

Hardships build your strength and enable you to move from being complacent to being more active in facing the challenges of life. We are being refined everyday, and that might take longer, but when all's said and done, we will become shining masterpieces of strength and valor. When we look back along the path of pain and suffering, we will find traces of little victories; when the last eight ounces of juices is served, I can breathe easily. Every day for the last twenty-four months of my daughter's Gerson therapy was really hard work. And every little victory was celebrated.

Ralph Waldo Emerson said, "We gain the strength of the temptation we resist." Powerful words. True enough, you increase your power in overcoming obstacles. Cancer could be one of the obstacles that blocks young peoples' dreams. How can you proceed when you're in bed, sick and dying? This concept is hard to grasp, and not easy to accept, but when we face these obstacles now, we regain the strength to keep us going. There were times that I almost gave in to the temptation of giving up the hope of healing, but when I looked at my daughter doing her part, it gave me the courage to keep moving on.

Today, challenges can be overcome. If we decide to win, we will surely win. You are bound for victory and not for defeat. Pastor Apollo C. Quiboloy, speaking to the International Youth Congress in Davao City on April 23, 2017, said, "Go, young people, for you are wired for success and not for defeat."

These words empower, motivate us to keep going even if the going is tough. Indeed, our help comes from above, the source of all that we can become and all that we can ever be. Healing comes from him; day in and day out, I keep reminding my daughter to seek God for help, "For with God nothing shall be impossible" (Luke 1:37 KJV).

The Story of Silvester Stallone, who, at the end of his struggles, said, "As long as you are alive, your life story is not yet over."

He was born paralyzed in the lower left part of his face, due to which his speech was slurred. At four, he was flat-footed, and put in dance school to overcome it. And at the age of twenty-four went to New York to pursue his dream of being an actor. He found nothing; all doors were closed to him.

He was so broke that he had to sleep in bus terminals for three weeks. He even had to sell his dog for $25 USD to survive, and out of desperation he started to make a pornographic film for $200 USD. One day, while watching a Muhammad Ali match, he got an idea for a screenplay, and he worked on the script for three days and three nights without sleep.

Things began to change. The producers were willing to pay him $350,000 USD for the script if he didn't act in the film. He refused big offers until one producer decided that he could play the lead role in the film. And guess what was the first thing he did after he received his money? He bought back his dog for $15,000 USD. After the huge success of the film, *Rocky*, the guy who slept at the bus terminal, sold his dog for $25, and made a film to survive, became a star.

In the life of Sylvester Stallone, endurance paid off; it was worth it to endure all the hardship for a noble desire to win. That burning desire within us that says no matter what it takes, we will do anything to achieve our dream. Yes, people who never give up pursue their wildest dreams (healing), with all their hearts. When we desire to change our lives, we don't see any obstacles that can deter us from obtaining those dreams.

Today, say to yourself: If they can do it, you too can do it; you can endure and enjoy life with teary eyes. The blood pumping in your heart like crazy tells you to never stop until you get what you really want.

When all's said and done, we are reminded of the fact that what lasts forever are those intangible, unseen rewards either here on earth, beneath, or up in heaven above. We can move forward; never retreat or surrender, for we will persist, no matter what.

## B: EMPOWERED THROUGH PERSISTENCE

When you start a journey, do not stop until you reach your destination. We cannot afford to give up, even when the going is tougher than we thought. We must move on, keep on, rallying behind the torch of victory. The weak give up so easily, even a few feet before the finish line. The losers are those who do not persist, those who do not persevere.

Gerson Therapy is a two-year program for which true commitment is needed for the desired results to come. We started on February 22, 2015 and continued until February 22, 2017. Every day, the thought of winning, mixed courage and was sprinkled with the steps that would bring my daughter complete healing. When excitement is created, supernatural strength begins to emerge. Deep within us is a burning desire that push us to do greater things, beyond our expectations.

We couldn't retreat from or back out of the Gerson protocol provided to us by Dr. Melvin Donato, a protocol that was regularly modified as my daughter's chemistry reports showed significant progress. Drums beat fast, and the sound of trumpets blew on the winds in a harmonious melody. Echoes of healing came barely three months with her Gerson therapy—her 9.25 cm swollen lymph nodes, the lump in her lungs, reduced to 2.24 cm. And after six months, there was no mass present on top of her lungs. Persistence brings victory and success, and we progressed towards our wish that complete healing was on the way.

We continued the journey in constant harmony. We measured every step, not minding what was ahead. Whether healing came or not, we remained totally steadfast. We were unhindered, even if the fear of death and struggle to live left her gasping for breath. Nothing could deter us; whether she lived or died, it didn't matter anymore. I found it difficult to tell my daughter that God owns her life; if God wanted her to live more years, it was up to him. Who am I to question His will?

Despite all the difficulty we're going through, there is an unseen hand that holds us all the time. There is an inward feeling of assurance and trust that, no matter what, you will accomplish what your mind conceived. The hand that leads the way guides and points you to total victory. He is a model of a true hero overcame obstacles, and no matter what he will guide you on a peaceful and safe path.

Lao Tzu tried to express that great things start from humble beginnings, He said, "A journey of a thousand miles begins with a single step" followed by another consistent step, continuously walking until the day comes when you reach your destination.

This book has been written so that we may find wisdom and understanding, step by step, guiding us to our own supercharged empowerment! There are many possibilities that await those who believe, and with greater faith, we will witness the manifestation of them. When we are endowed with power, the destiny of man lies in our hands. We are equipped with majesty, crowned with His glory, that of the everlasting God who has rescued us in every difficulty. But we must learn to wait, to wait patiently. Are we able to do that? Please, let's move along the path of empowerment through patience.

## C: EMPOWERED THROUGH PATIENCE

The longer the waiting, the greater the blessing. Your strength is renewed every step of the way. The challenging part of life is patient waiting; too many people don't have the courage to wait. They would rather rush, the easy way, taking the path to chemotherapy and making drastic decisions based on their feelings. Pain produces discomfort; we want to feel good, but we don't have the patience to wait for healing. Patience is a virtue that can only be achieved with tons of waiting; our capacity to bear and endure hardships creates a patient heart.

Waiting increases our strength. With bended knee, we do not resort to regression. They who wait upon the forces of goodness will regain strength they cannot imagine. They will be renewed with awesome power, they will walk and not faint along the way, and they will run and not get tired.

For twenty four solid months, we were taught to wait and see what the Lord God would manifest in our midst. Our challenges came with certain purpose, undisclosed to the receiver, and it will bring about lasting monumental change within us, and we will never be the same. Everything has a purpose, and that includes empowerment through pain, and agony through waiting. Waiting produces patience and hope, which fuels continuity, which energizes the weary, so they can keep moving on. It also produces courage and fearlessness, even when the evidence is unclear. Though there were some significant results, we still do not know what the future would hold. Do we manifest weakness in waiting? Not at all. We win while waiting. We gain strength, developing an unyielding fighting spirit that will not allow the option of giving up.

There were times when we became impatient because our expectations were not met; we didn't see the results we wanted to see. The fear of dying engulfed our wounded soul. Makes us impatient, and it's not normal to say, "Thank you, God, for the pain," or "Praise God, I am in pain." Can you rejoice while you are facing impending death? Can you be happy even when your oncologist says you have three months to live without chemotherapy and one year to live if you go through it? The bottom line is that you still die sooner or later. We learn to wait for healing; the Creator, in His time, will show us miracles. We cannot command God to heal us. During this waiting time, we gain strength as we learn the lesson of patience during excruciating pain. We need the grace of God to go through the process of healing.

Every step of the way is a process of revelation. There are things in life learned only through hardship and pain. Nevertheless, if we become more aware, more sensitive to the prompting by which the Creator allows us to be healed, then every day is a day of praising, rejoicing, and thanksgiving. Apostle Paul said, in everything give thanks: for this is the will of God" (1 Thessalonians 5:18 KJV). Wow, give thanks when you're in pain? Praise Him when you are suffering? Pray when you don't have the energy to pray? Yes. When God says "everything," it includes every detail in life; there is no exception, whether in good or bad times.

We are motivated to trust Him whose power is greater than ours, "for greater is He that is in you than he that is in the world" (1 John 4:4 KJV). Truly, God is bigger than our troubles, higher than mountaintops, and stronger than a lion. We keep believing, and we remain faithful. We keep hoping—it may take too long, but believe me, it's worth the waiting anyways. For in waiting, there is a renewal of strength, there is refilling of energy. It is when we go through the beating and shaking of life that we learn to handle hardships and become stronger. We never give in to shallowness and lightness of faith; instead, we go deeper and higher.

Patience must go through severe testing, making sure it's tempered with the longest waiting time. There are times that we flare up in a display of anger because we lack patience. We lose control of our temper when we do not learn to patiently wait in prayer. There are times in life that we must go through this waiting time so that we may gain wisdom and strength to move on.

Writing this book involved a lot of waiting. There were times I was seated and waiting for someone, waiting for my turn at the bank, and waiting for my queue at the medical clinic. Yes, time cannot be wasted—either I read a book, or I was writing something that I believed would inspire someone to live.

Lastly, let me add these very important words from Isaiah 40:31 (KJV): "For they that wait upon the Lord shall renew their strength; they shall mount up with wings as eagles; they shall run and not be weary; and they shall walk, and not faint." A promise is given to those who wait upon the Lord. Their strength will be renewed. There will be a time of renewal and refreshment. They will fly like eagles, which soar during stormy weather, and they will fly against the stormy wind until they reach higher than the wind.

You run, but you never will get tired if you keep running; strength is continuously given. Keep running the race of faith, for in due time we reap the harvest if we don faint, Isaiah the prophet said, "They shall walk and not faint." There is a regular supply of spiritual nourishment that revitalizes and rejuvenates your spiritual being. It pays to wait. When we have the right focus, our path will be clearer than we thought.

## D: *EMPOWERED THROUGH FOCUS*

People who never get distracted are focus-driven people. We lack focus when we do not see things clearly, when our vison is dark and blurry. Most of our mistakes occur when we do not see things clearly and make decisions based on what we hardly see. Our perception—whether it's clear or obstructed—will show the cause and effect of our decision. When it is not crystal clear, do not plan, and refrain from making comments or conclusions. To do so may cost you a fortune.

Being focused first means your eyes is set on one thing that you are interested in accomplishing? What makes you wake up excited in the morning? When we are not interested in what we are doing, we drag our feet; we are not motivated, right? We just exist, and we have no life. There is no meaning in what we do. We have wasted our time.

Our main objective within this two-year period was to focus on doing what was right every day, on not making any deviation from or variation on the set protocol. Healing is about timing, precision, focus, and overcoming obstructions.

"Focus" can be defined as "the state or quality of having or producing clear visual definition." It is when you know your why. Why are you doing what you're doing now? What are you trying to accomplish in life? Do you have a clear understanding of your direction? When you visualize why you are doing what you are doing now, you begin to spend time enhancing your skills, preparing yourself for developing all related plans. Then, and only then, are you geared towards succeeding.

We must pay close attention to every detail. We cannot be complacent. Closely follow up, evaluating and carrying out every step towards excellence and perfection. When we started Gerson therapy, we had a lot of preparations to make; the kitchen had to be devoid of salt, oil, sugar, white or whole-wheat flour, and some spices. The spices that are allowed must be organic. The only oil my daughter could use was cold-pressed flaxseed oil, stored in a black container; a clear container destroys the enzymes.

During those months, there were a lot of people who were trying to divert us from Gerson therapy. They made promises of healing. They thought they had better ideas. If we listened to them, at the end of the day we regretted having followed their pernicious ways.

While writing this, I have an inner sensation, a feeling urging me to share what I learned. Sometimes I hesitate, because I think that readers might not see what I want them to see or feel what I want them to feel. I am writing all my thoughts, wishing that one day someone reads my book and finds comfort in each page. Yes, this is the reason for my existence—that I might lead people to find true happiness and live a meaningful life. This is my mission. This is my goal. This is the reason you are reading the pages of this book. It is for your guidance. May you find your way to the path of your empowerment.

I wish to share valuable lessons in the pages of this book, which is filled with wisdom and life-giving words. It is encouragement for the weary, a guide toward healing, and a compass to guide us along the way. A life that recorded in the annals of human history, telling an awesome story of a meaningful journey. Let this be material you can use to enlighten those in your sphere of influence, bringing change to people's lives from within, eventually a living testimony for everyone to see.

Lastly, we do not look only from within to what is going on out there, but also outside ourselves.

# CHAPTER 5

## SUPERCHARGING THE BODY

### A: *SUPERCHARGING THROUGH CLEANSING*

I went to Davao City, Philippines and meet Dr. Jaymaima Coching, PhD, a naturopathic doctor who focuses on parasitology, on August 29, 2017. Her basic premise, when it comes to any kind of disease, is that we humans have monsters within us and we are not aware that they truly exist; to name a few, she mentions hookworms, tapeworms, and other parasites that live in the human body. She believes that the cause of many diseases is parasites. She cited, as one example, that sometimes when a person has poor eyesight, it is because the person has a tapeworm covering the eye. The need for detoxification is essential. She also produces the product that resolves these issues. Deworming is her call, her advocacy. Her battle cry, **"Annihilate the Monster within you."**

The physical weakness we sometimes were going through occurred because we didn't have any detoxification at all in our lives. The Monster or the worms grows bigger, longer, and more active; all the nutrients in the food we eat go directly to feeding this monster. It is an ugly picture, but this is how it looks when we do not properly cleanse our system from these worms. We must be proactive with our health, as our bodies have had garbage dumped in them for so many years. The body must get rid of these unwanted monsters and go back to total health and wellness.

Gerson therapy also includes detox in their protocol, my daughter was given deworming drops to accompany her green juices. My daughter's protocol also included detoxifying using a coffee enema.

For the first six months, this coffee enema was done five times a day. It was not easy for Hannah to go back and forth to the washroom, lying down the floor sideways while she pushed the little outlet tube into her anus, eight to ten inches deep. Yeah, you might be saying, "Wow, I could not do that!" But we had to do what needed to be done for healing to happen. (Step-by-step guide to coffee enema: Appendix)

We don't plan just for the sake of planning; we implement our plan with all diligence. We have the capability to make things happen. We were focused, with a single-minded approach: every day we moved with calculated timing, and exact measurements. We followed her Gerson protocol, doing what was right. Involve yourself in every detail of, you must see how things work to be able to make things right, from the very start to the very end.

When a person puts his whole heart into achieving something and is passionate about it, miracles can happen. All your strength and creativity put together will surely do wonders—I mean spectacular miracles. In every aspect of our lives, we must believe in ourselves, knowing that wisdom is freely given to us, yes, free of charge.

## B: SUPERCHARGING THROUGH PHYSICAL ACTIVITY

Our physical healing begins from within. It is our faith that moves mountains. We can do the impossible: "Greater is he that is in you, than he that is in the world" (I John 4:4 KJV). First and foremost, our tools and machinery are spiritual in nature. They are not physical; rather, they are the supernatural work of the unseen spiritual armies whose work it is to make things good and defy evil. The enemy of our soul comes to kill, harm, and destroy, but will not succeed. We are engaged, and we cannot turn our backs and quit. We must move forward in victorious conquest.

The daily routine in purchasing food, the food preparation, juicing, homemaking, and sleepless nights of caregiving, continued for six hundred days. It takes patience and strong faith that what we were doing would make a difference. I kept on reminding myself that it could be done, that she would survive this ordeal; we could defeat death. This therapy works. We could not be defeated; we could only win when we were determined, dedicated, devoted, and diligent. This was the burning resolve kept fueling us.

I have been traveling during the writing of this book. I was in Asia, visited Macau for few days, and then went back to Hong Kong. The people coming to Macau, which is the Las Vegas of Asia, came with a burning desire to win. I interviewed some of those who worked there, and they mentioned that people bring luggage filled not with clothes and fancy stuff but rather with cash. They said you can't imagine how much people spend to satisfy their burning desire for gambling, hoping to win but ending up losing. When they run out of cash, Chinese people will go to the bank and withdraw again and again, expecting that anytime soon they will win. That burning desire to win is what made my daughter and I win the fight against cancer.

We can conquer our greatest challenge, climb the highest mountain without fear of any danger. Our fearless spirit motivates us to go beyond what the human imagination can conceive of and this is kind of empowered people we became, people who will never stop inspiring others, empowering everyone who is drawn near.

The captivating influence of a leader who does not see a half-empty glass, a leader who rather sees what a half-full glass can accomplish. This is a person tempered by seasoned, timeless experience, whose wisdom is more than that of the gurus of his time. He is full of knowledge, wisdom, and understanding, open to possibilities rather than the difficulties he himself cannot overcome. We will be the people we create ourselves to be. There is nothing that we put our entire mind to plan and create that cannot be done. We must make sure that whatever we do, we do it with all our might, with all our strength—nothing less than our best. We must aim at excellence in everything that we do, not mediocrity.

During those trying moments, God made us strong, both spiritually and physically. Barely three months into her Gerson therapy, my daughter invited me to go out for a walk at Holland Park. She had begun regaining her strength and walking became her daily exercise. She gained strength over time as we worked together towards emotional, spiritual, and physical healing.

We truly felt that in being part of something great, we made ourselves involved in a very rewarding work. We were proactive in the work of bringing lasting change to both the physical and the spiritual dimensions of our lives. Bearing the marks of perfection, we progressed through temporary setbacks and discomfort, which brought changes to our inner mental and emotional stability. Strength is found during struggles and sorrow; the irony is that power is gained through weakness and pain.

## C: SUPERCHARGED WHEN RESTED

*Selah* is frequently used in the psalms of King David. This word means to pause, meditate, contemplate, and evaluate, then start afresh with a new template. The word *psalms* in Hebrew means songs; in singing, you must follow the time signature, the pitch, the breathing, and the value of each musical notes to be able to come up with a beautiful, harmonious sound. In life, we play a lot of music; we sing songs, and whether these are out of tune or in tune depends upon us as singers.

Do not allow stressful work to drain you. Work will always be there. Deadlines that should always be met demand time and attention. To succeed and survive, you've got to have some time for a meditative pause. Meditative pauses are essential in our daily living; they're like taking a deep breath to be able to take in more fresh air. In meditation, we focus on the higher cause, understanding the deeper meaning of the things we do and why we do them. A sense of purpose defines us—a wider perspective and deep-rooted whys—and most of all a higher vision of life, a greater horizon.

Contemplation is a practice of deeper reflective thought and action—looking on something for a long period of time, a continuous consideration of the plans you have in life. You look at the beginning and the end, organizing facts in between with deeper thought and consideration. This is the evaluation process by which we gauge ourselves according to the standards and expectations we set, weighing everything into the balance to see where we realistically stand, and then providing ourselves various options, models, and templates for implementation.

We must test, look at the rear view, the side view, the upward view, and the front view. Write your observations; take note of the changes you need to take immediate action. Do not procrastinate; do what needs to be done without further delay. Procrastination delays growth, stagnates and dries you up, and decreases your momentum. Do what you need to do in no time at all; do not leave for tomorrow what can be done today. When we fail to maximize our time, our money, resources, manpower, and opportunity diminish. When it's gone, it's gone for eternity.

Stressful operations can be eliminated when the proper coordination and communication of those involved has been strictly followed. Our assumptions and presupposition are not always correct; facts and figures will not lie. Accuracy is important, and when we are accurate, every number fit into the puzzle. Smoother operations are accomplished with thorough quality control from point A to Z; otherwise, everything will mess up, and progress will be stunted.

Learn to be calm. Nervousness will take away our focus, will push us away from understanding. Then it will only make us more worried than ever before. There are things that, no matter how we try to correct them, it seems they don't go away. Learn the path of peace. Take a walk, exercise, join yoga sessions, go to the swimming pool, take a brisk walk, run, jump, ride your bike, and make yourself mobile and active.

Follow a program; you gain power by putting yourself back on the right track and accomplishing more than you aimed for.

## *EXERCISE:*

1. Take a break, meditate two to three times a day.

2. Sit in a quiet room away from any disturbance.

3. A meditative prayer is healthy.

Close your eyes and your mind. Focus on one object.

## D: REMEMBER KARMA

Steven Covey once said **"Sow a thought, reap an action; sow an action, reap a habit; sow a habit, reap a character; sow a character, reap a destiny."**

I am astounded when people say they don't care what they say, that it's just words. Words are powerful: they can bring joy, induce suffering, divide families, cause war, divide a nation. Words can create anything. That's how powerful words are. Pastor Apollo C. Quiboloy of the Kingdom of Jesus Christ mentioned numerous times quoting this this verse from scripture: "The words that I speak unto you, they are spirit, and they are life" (John 6:63 KJV). These are powerful words that mean words are an immaterial expression that can produce a tangible reality.

When we clearly understand this, it means that reality is conceived in the womb of our imagination, and then we speak those conceptions out into reality. The words spoken will become action because a person's thoughts become his reality. When these actions are repeated, they become a habit, a normal disposition, and a regular way of doing things. Surprisingly, you don't have to say anything; it naturally comes out. A person doesn't even have to try anymore; it automatically comes out as a natural reaction. Why? Because it's now become a habit.

Going through the process of healing with words is crucial to the outcome; our words will either encourage or discourage, like the friends of Job in the Bible. Our daily confession, or if I may call it a mantra, will bring about an undeniably positive outcome. For 600 days we confessed healing and declared victory over the challenges of every day. Our mantra brought us life, our confession increased our faith, and our actions coordinated how we felt and what we said. When you do that, you are creating destiny; you are putting together the unseen materials of healing. You are putting together reasons for the Almighty to grant your request.

In the same manner, in the body, when we keep feeding ourselves junk food, acidic, non-alkaline food, we'll end up either in an emergency room or the morgue. Keep stealing, and one day you'll be caught and end up in jail. In short, our actions will show our possible destination. The same principle is true in the physical and the spiritual dimension.

We must do what is right always, for we get what we have given, harvest what we have sown. That's the law of karma. The lone voice in the modern wilderness of information technology has declared and proclaimed the words of the Almighty, saying that "There is a way that seems right unto a man, but the end thereof are the ways of death" (Proverbs 14:12 KJV). Adam, our first parent, never realized the devastating effect of rejecting the words of the Creator. Instead, he entertained the words of the devil, thereby disobeying and going against the almighty Father's perfect will.

Because of Adam and Eve's actions the people of the world—regardless of their race, language, religion, culture, the color of their skin—became evil, egoistic, and disobedient, unhealthy and sick in both the physical and spiritual dimensions. That brought war and disease, destroyed the environment, and changed the universal laws of nature, bringing this world in which we are now living almost to great ruin. Sooner or later, we reap the consequences of the choices we have made. When we make a peaceful revolutionary change, first from within, followed by the outward actions we take every day, we can turn this planet from devastation to paradise once again.

It is a fact that the world we're living in is a by-product of decisions made in the past; a lot of the time we cannot alter them and will have to ride with the waves or dance with the music of irresponsibility and callousness. We must make our choices right, our words right, our actions right. Then we will produce the right stuff, begin declaring the word of healing, and wellness will come. Our way of life has changed even the words we speak; it has transformed our inner beings. Speak blessings. Parents start to speak blessing among our children; stop cursing them, no matter what they have done. Children start speaking blessings to your parents, no matter what they have done. Leaders bless your people, no matter what they have accomplished, whether it meets your criterion or not.

The diseases of our body are by-products of what we have eaten in the past, the lifestyle we practice, our hobbies; the harmful activity we have done in the past, the more we will receive the by-product of the actions we've taken. Even the apostle Paul emphasized this, and said,

"Finally, brethren, whatsoever things are true, whatsoever things are honest, whatsoever things are just, whatsoever things are pure, whatsoever things are lovely, whatsoever things are of good report; if there be any virtue and if there be any praise, think on these things" (Philippians 4:8 KJV).

You immerse your mind in these beautiful words of truth, which produce positive thoughts, giving you the necessary mindset to do the will of the Father of all Spirits, our Lord, Jesus Christ.

If you desire a beautiful tomorrow, start planting the seeds today, for they will grow over time and bring about a wonderful future. Amen!

# CHAPTER 6

## SUPERCHARGING THE SPIRIT

### A: MANIFESTING AN UNWAVERING FAITH

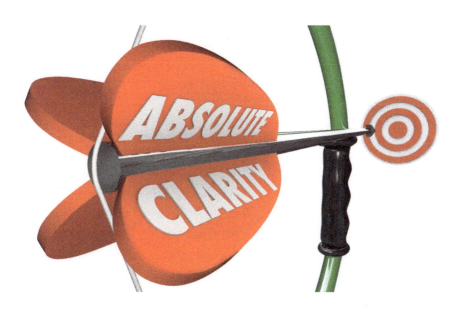

*"When you go beyond your fear, then victory is infinite!"*

— The Son, Pastor Apollo C. Quiboloy

We are afraid of the unknown we may have many speculations, nevertheless truth will come to the surface. Fear will cause a mental blockage and will make you less effective and less efficient with what you are doing.

Faith energizes the weak and the faint-hearted; it fuels our mind with determination to keep on moving on. Nothing in this world can surpass what faith can do. It can build huge edifices, move mountains, and do the impossible. There are moments in our lives when we face challenges, sometimes beyond our capability. Dealing with cancer is not an easy thing to manage, for it involves the body, the soul, the spirit, and finances.

A lot of people are stuck in fear: fear of what an outcome will be, fear of being criticized, fear rather than belief. They become paranoid. Fear paralyzes our faith, which causes us to stumble and fall, diminishing our power to create. Fear will pull us down, instead of lifting us in faith to the highest pinnacle of success. "Fear paralyzes but our faith energizes."

These are several principles of which we should continuously remind ourselves. We must believe in a life of confidence, abundance, prosperity, and resourcefulness—a life not lesser than your potential, the highest degree of your inner being. Keep believing, keep trusting, for greater things come to those who believe than to those who remain in unbelief. Miracles happen to those who trust and keep believing.

Faith is a magic word in this journey of life. Faith is when we believe in something beyond our human understanding, stepping into the unknown with courage, not knowing what the future holds. Faith is our resonance with the Almighty, that is deep within us. Whatever it takes, you never will regret faith, because even if your faith is smaller than a mustard seed, it can do wonders and miracles.

This is what holds us together during these trying moments: our faith. Our faith might be tested, but we will remain faithful, even when things are not working according to our expectations. We must stay faithful, believing that whatever happens, words and action remain consistent. Nothing matters in our daily lives more than doing what is right; doing what is right will eventually lead us to a better way of life.

Believing is amazingly wonderful. Faith makes things happen, allows the impossible to become possible, makes things come into reality out of nothing. An active faith can bring about supernatural manifestations of divine work, acted out by mere human beings whose faith is deeply rooted in the words of God. His words become a reality—a tangible, visible reality, seen by our human eyes. Faith creates the answer you have formed in the womb of your thoughts and imagination. If we want healing, healing should be conceived in the womb of our mind and be allowed to grow to fruition.

Fear is produced by our minuscule power, but faith focuses on the gargantuan power of the Almighty God. We win our battles not by our tiny power but rather with the colossal power of God. His greatness can do gigantic work in our midst, but only when we believe. On January 25, 2015, words of faith, from Pastor Apollo C Quiboloy, were whispered in my daughter's ears, "You are healed. Take it by faith, without wavering. Believe you are healed, and you will be healed." These words became the guiding mental mantra for my daughter and me.

Indeed, there is power in believing, for when we put our hearts and minds to something, the whole universe joins in an awesome chorus, singing the marching tune that fills our hearts with courage to fight and move forward. There is no room for cowards, or for those who retreat when it's time to fight. The voice of excitement roars and shouts of victory, filling up the empty space. We saw faith at work in every aspect of my daughter's medical examination; we saw daily progress and healing.

We would like to thank God for using the Executive Pastor of the Kingdom of Jesus Christ, the leader of the Kingdom of Jesus Christ, the name above every name, whose headquarters is in Davao City, Philippines. He is known to be a man of great faith and believes faith can move mountains, making everything a possibility. At the writing of this book, the Kingdom of Jesus Christ celebrates thirty-three years of fruitful, bountiful, mightily blessed ministry, the orchestration of the Father Almighty, honoring his faith, together with a host of full-time miracle workers who held his hand, making the impossible possible.

The awesome truth is that faith is the victory for those who believe all things are possible. There is no reason to fear, neither doubt nor despair, for faith conquers your deepest, innermost fear. Our strength is refueled by the words of wisdom we always hear, words of eternal life. Cling to that which is good, learn to always trust and obey His words, for in obedience there are blessings we surely will enjoy.

We conquer negativity with courage, defeating faithlessness, indifference, and inactivity. We become zealous with everything that we do, exercising our will to do what is right. That is where we gain the strength to neither falter nor fall, standing firm for what is good and eschewing evil once and for all.

Passing through San Francisco, USA for Hong Kong, China bound for Vancouver, Canada in September of 2017, was amazing. I looked at tourists from different parts of the globe, taking photos and having a good time. I ate at Chart House at Pier 39, facing Alcatraz's far distant shore, which reminded me of what the American prison island used to be. It has become a tourist destination; you can book a night's stay on the island. The fate of every person who did time in this solitary prison in the middle of the sea is horrifying, yet the escape of three prisoners showed that nothing is insurmountable and that even a walled island prison cannot stop people who believe they can escape.

Alcatraz was their fate, but there is struggle within them for freedom from imprisonment. Their gesture of belief, craftsmanship, planning, and leadership in putting together a way to freedom. While others thought it was impossible, it took just one man to say, "It is possible only when you believe." You've got to believe in miracles to come, for in believing, you please the Almighty to act on your behalf.

## B: MANIFESTING A BLESSED HOPE

When I wake up in the morning, the journey of life excites me, and I am full of hope and endless expectations. Our individual, unique journey in life leaves us memorable stories to tell; some may be sad, a lot may be very challenging. Yet each of these stories has chapters filled with unquestionable experiences of hope. Every episode is mingled with colorful shades of light, the shadows of some distant past. It could be an exciting journey, tearful and painful, or it could be a journey of triumphant entry to endless possibility.

Every step of the way is unknown. We can look upon it with some clarity only when we have experienced the entirety of the journey, only to realize life has been wasted, that mistakes can no longer be corrected. We take wisdom from the lessons learned on this journey. Hope makes our journey more exciting, giving us a sense of direction. No matter what we are going through, hope is a bright, shining light along the darkened path.

I remember the day my daughter called me on the phone while I was in Hong Kong. She was sobbing, while I was listening to her cracking voice, filled with worries and in the depths of despair, I sighed and prayed to God to give me strength that I might be able to bring her hope. It wasn't easy, receiving the news of sickness and possible death of a loving daughter.

You might have shattered dreams, which depress you all the time. It could be that your business is on the brink of collapsing. Or maybe you feel everything seems unfair and no one really cares, a difficult feeling when you need someone, and you have no one with whom to share. With no one to turn to or listen to your side of the story, the feeling of loneliness engulfs your heart and fear increases, immobilizing your whole body with terror. You have nowhere to go for help, but looking up, you see an angelic host of heaven come to rescue you. There are times when you don't expect a rescue to come, but then help surfaces out of nowhere, providing solutions everywhere.

When you know who you know, when you know who He is, then you feel that deep hope of belonging and security. A lot of time, it is not what you know that matters; rather, it is who you know that really matters most. Our expectations will never be frustrated in the hands that made the world, the one who created you and the universe around you. The galaxies manifest His vastness in power; all creation cannot ignore the power of the great Almighty Creator.

With the thought of who Jesus Christ is, we forget who we are; magnetized by His appealing presence, we are flooded with His awesome love. The agony He endured and the pain He suffered it seems then hope was gone, all heavenly hosts were saddened when He died for man. He went through His life and death with no fear, no surrender, no retreat; the sacrifice He made became my pattern to emulate.

When I heard my daughter's news, I silently prayed for inner strength, and my daughter shared, in her cracking voice, that she had been diagnosed with stage three Hodgkin lymphoma, and that she would have to undergo twelve chemotherapy sessions. The doctor had mentioned no other option.

It wasn't easy, but there was an inner power from within my soul, giving me hope. Yes, it was hope in the middle of turmoil, an assurance that no matter what, the will of the Creator always prevails. The promise was not for a smooth journey. Rather, the promise was, "I will never leave you nor forsake you" (Deuteronomy 31:6 NIV). This is a promise that will transform people who live according to its expectations. What we ask, and desires come to fruition not on our terms and conditions or on our set dates but are rather the work and orchestration of divine intervention.

My daughter's oncologist insisted that she have twelve chemotherapy sessions, but Hannah refused, saying, "If I die, I'd rather die without pain." We had the help of my daughter's regional director at Teavana, who introduced us to Gerson therapy; she'd also had cancer when she was twenty-four years old she same age as my daughter. She was so generous, giving my daughter a gift of books by Dr. Max Gerson and Dorothy Gerson, and a heavy-duty Champion juicer machine. She is indeed a good-hearted person, full of love and compassion for my daughter.

In 2017, after twenty-four months of Gerson therapy, which involved strenuous juicing, twenty-four different supplements, exercises, dietary discipline, and spiritual renewal, my daughter was declared cancer-free after her PET scan and related medical evaluation. Indeed, there is hope in a hopeless situation; there is an answer amid unavoidable circumstances. When you learn to see through the spiritual eyes of faith, the God of great wonders will manifest provisions that will never come too late.

Learning to believe, with full expectations that the universe will join us on our quest for greater heights and eternal bliss, is a key to hope. There are unseen forces waiting to unleash their blessings, but only when we believe. Disbelief will lead us astray from the path of goodness, wellness, and righteousness. For when we begin to falter, our faith is small. When our faith is small, we have nothing to hope for. Faith increases our expectations, energizes us from within, and motivates us to create positive things.

There is no reason to be faithless and hopeless; there are thousands of reasons to be full of vibrant faith and hope. Consider the inner core of your values; stop focusing your eyes on negative words and vibrations. Learn to look up to the skies, to the beauty and grandeur no one can deny. Look around beautiful British Columbia with her rolling terrain, beautiful rivers, and parks filled with tall, strong, aged pine trees. See the gorgeous scenery, undeniable in its majesty and beauty.

When you lose hope, it is because of yourself. There is no one else to blame. When you learn to be thankful for the things you're blessed with, then you will never complain. Why? Because you have so much to enjoy, even every drop of Vancouver rain. Yes, we are a city where it rains so much, but we love it; it fills British Columbia with towering trees and green pastures.

There are always reasons to be happy, to be patient with each other, to love one another. In this, we fulfill the law of the universe. For when we give love, we beget more love. When we sow kindness, we reap like-mindedness. When we learn to share hope and inspiration, we get encouragement we cannot imagine. Yes, everyone needs someone who empowers them, who exhales goodness, tender-heartedness, understanding, and willingness to suffer for their sake.

Two months after my daughter's diagnosis, Pastor Apollo C. Quiboloy visited Vancouver for his "King is Coming" tour concert at the beautiful Vancouver Convention Centre, which had been built for the 2008 Winter Olympics. I cannot forget that night. When the altar call was made, my daughter joined the throng of people lining up to be blessed by the good pastor. It was an act of faith.

When her turn came, I whispered into the ear of the Appointed Son of God, "She is my daughter who is suffering from cancer." Pastor Apollo moved his hand to my daughter's neck, laying his hand on her chest, where the 9.25 cm lymph node tumor was growing. There was an awesome reverential feeling of the presence of some powerful force that moved through the congregation. Right after the worship service, my daughter began testifying, revealing what she'd felt upon the anointing she'd received from the Appointed Son of God. She was filled with ecstatic excitement, saying, **"I felt the touch of God and saw in his eyes the compassion of Jesus Christ."**

I was so deeply blessed, and her brother with us.

Yes, there is hope, for this generation is so blessed. Indeed, the touch and prayers of the Appointed Son of God were heard. Two years after my daughter's oncologist had given her three months to live, at the time of writing these pages, she spent three months touring Europe together with her dear brother. Some of these photos were taken during her tour.

## C: MANIFESTING HIGH MOTIVATION

Highly motivated people are those leaders who will not allow any obstacle to stop them. A well-focused person will never be distracted by anything; no bad weather will deter them from the task they have set out to accomplish.

Who cannot allow any obstacle to stop them from reaching their goals? Those who accomplish things never give up; rather, they become more highly motivated in achieving goals. There are amazing stories of people who, through their strong will, were able to reach greater heights.

We will become what we think we are. We can do what our mind and heart set out to do. Inner desire mobilizes the timid and inspires them to keep moving on, inch by inch, and to reach the level of success they set their minds to, with amazing results. What the mind can conceive can be achieved.

The life that highly motivates me is the life of Pastor Apollo C. Quiboloy, who, against all odds, follows his calling without doubt, fulfilling what his heart and mind set to do. It is an inward motivational force that drives him to accomplish great things in life. He is a person who is full of faith, filled with love and compassion, whose mandate is beyond the physical realm, of a higher spiritual dimension.

He is so highly motivated that no matter what happens, he is committed only to what is pleasing to God, who called him. You cannot bribe him, nor does he seek favors from anyone; rather, he is a giver, a philanthropist, a builder, an educator, an engineer, a designer, an environmentalist, an advocate of peace, a golfer, a basketball player, and most of all a life-transforming preacher, who proclaims from the depths of his heart the message that will change the course of human history. He is bold and never afraid of what the opposition will say; he is fully committed to pleasing God. He is a person who has beautified the earth by helping with the rebuilding and reforestation of the foothills of Mount Apo, restoring the balance of our ecosystem. He is an inspiration, with a following of 6.5 million in two thousand cities in two hundred countries around the world. He is an awesome planner, programmer, financier, employer, producer, and a father to more than two thousand children at his school, the Jose Maria College, who are on full academic scholarships.

As a philanthropist, he established the Children's Joy Foundation, Inc. whose mission is to provide physical, emotional, intellectual, and spiritual transformation to poor, abandoned, and destitute children all over the world. This charity feeds, clothes, shelters, and educates children to help them become healthy, balanced, well-mannered, and spiritually mature adults. The foundation is opening more branches in many countries, addressing the needs of those who are hurting the most. Yes, his is a very inspiring life, indeed. Please visit www.childrensjoyfoundation.org, www.cjfcanada.ca and www.apollocquiboloy.com/www.kingdomofjesuschrist.org.

# D: MANIFESTING TRUE, LASTING HAPPINESS

*"Lasting happiness is achieved not through anything physical but everything spiritual."*

—Pastor Apollo C. Quiboloy

Happiness is one of the most sought-after inner qualities, for it brings joy and fulfillment to a person's life. Yet so many people have the wrong notions about how they can be happy. They resort to some temporary relief that provides them emptiness, if not addiction of a certain sort, instead.

They fail to see their value, their contribution to humanity—a sense of purpose and direction. When we know the reason for our existence, we live a life that is more fulfilling. Happiness is also produced by doing everything you do to the best of your ability, doing an excellent job. When a person ceases to socialize with happy people and hangs out with narrow-minded, negative, unhappy people, then he becomes like them.

True happiness is made. It is created, and can be developed, enhanced, and made perfect. Fill your inner being with spiritual values that last forever, inner strength that sustains you in times of need and during the surprises of life. Seen with your beautiful smile, and felt through the vibrations of your emotions, feelings of joy reverberate and echo from your innermost soul.

A never-ending overflowing of happiness, during the best or even the saddest experiences of life, is not governed by the physical realm. By overcoming natural human tendencies and entering a spiritual spectrum that others do not dare to enter, gutsy risk-takers go beyond their mental understanding, accomplish things beyond human reason, and attain what seems impossible. When we take these steps, we join ourselves to those who dare to be thankful and happy, even in the most adverse of situations.

There is real happiness in doing things with all our might, with strength and vigor, knowing that success is given to those who seek and work towards reaching it. The disappointments they may face and struggles they might be embroiled in do not really matter to those who are truly happy—their joy remains the same regardless of their physical reality. They are unmoved by their circumstances and determined to move on, no matter what.

Happiness also comes from doing what you love, what is dear to your heart, and what gives meaning to your existence. When a person does what he loves, he can accomplish great things. Great exploits produce real happiness when they come from love. Be happy with what you do, love what you do, and accomplish what makes you happy in life.

Openness to change is essential to achieving real and lasting happiness. Be ready to amend your ways. If things do not work the way you planned, change your method, change your strategies, change your attitude, and keep moving on. Do not stop. You can rest for a while, but you cannot be off track. Keep moving on, keep pressing on, and keep smiling. The end might be so near, and the greatest reward will be achieved; quitting should not be an option.

Move along the path of light, undeterred by the oppressing force of darkness. The Master's call will be, "Well done, my son. Enter the success of all your labors." We are called to accomplish the very purpose of our birth. No one can do it for us. We've got to complete the mission of our existence.

Fulfillment of purpose brings endless happiness, an atmosphere of true meaning, of success. What defines you? What will the epitaph above your grave read? What books will recount your story? How will you be remembered? How would you like people to talk on the day of your funeral? It all will depend on the kind of person you have created yourself to be. A happy old man or a grumpy, selfish old man? You alone can define who you will be.

A quest for lasting joy and the true meaning of happiness cannot be found in a bank account or the pages of one's portfolio, in titles of real estate, or in superficial accomplishments. Rather, it is found in the heart, in the very innermost soul, where true happiness lies serenely, tranquilly, the pristine essence of never-ending joy.

# CHAPTER 7

## EMPOWERING MY SOCIAL LIFE

### A: *MANIFESTED THROUGH FALLEN WALLS*

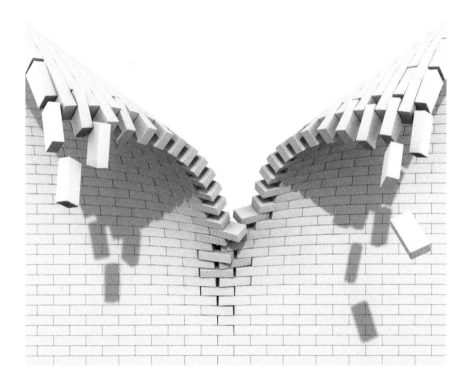

When we decided to push thru with my daughter's protocol there was not only a feeling of being alienated from the support of organizations that advocated chemotherapy but also of being deprived of the freedom to make our choices. The process was not easy; it took my daughter hours and hours of discussion with her oncologists, who wanted her to complete the twelve sessions. We were accused of using quack medicine, as Dr. Max Gerson was branded in this way during his struggle for recognition from the medical society in the 1940s.

When my daughter had her first chemo session, different organizations called us, opening their doors. There was a family whose son had the same cancer as my daughter who contacted me, in case we needed moral support. Yes, we received enormous support, but when we made a paradigm shift each door began to close, and we received no more calls, no more support. We feel somewhat outcast, deprived from any protection, with no back-up from an institution.

However, we remained steadfast; we held on to our hope and expectation that the decision we made was the right one. There was opposition. It wasn't accepted with open arms; even my cousin, who is a medical doctor, was not happy with our decision.

In the medical field, the conventions of modern medicine have changed our traditional ways. The enema is one of the oldest ways of cleansing and fine-tuning the body; even during the time of the Roman Empire, enemas were used. With the Gerson therapy, as I mentioned in Chapter 4 – Supercharging Your Body, coffee enemas are part of the protocol. This method began after World War II, when soldiers who were accidentally given coffee enemas instead of water felt way better than those who received only water, from the military museum inn UK, coffee enemas are mentioned in the World War II 1944 RAMC training manual.

The freedom to choose should be given to patients to choose which path they want to take in the process of healing their diseases, especially cancer? As my daughter and I experienced when we were given the only option, nothing else matters except chemotherapy. Medical practices have been modernized, with the sacrifice of some traditional ways that are effective, and which could be integrated into advanced technological medical practices. When I was talking to my daughter's oncologist, I encouraged him to integrate conventional and traditional, natural ways. Dr. X replied, "I cannot gamble with it with my medical license." It seems that there are medical associations that prohibit such integrative practices. During the first few days of my daughter's two chemo sessions, I gave her an extra dose of spirulina and soursop fruit tea (Guyabano)

The walls of selfishness are no longer relevant in hearts filled with unconditional love and commitment. It is in unselfishness that we extend a helping hand, even to the farthest corners of the globe, making lives better, bringing change. Yes, a heart and a hand, for a desire kept in secret with no plans for execution is futile and useless. A good heart can cause a hand to move and extend help wherever there is a need.

Breaking down the walls that separate us—we might ask how thick they are and if we can tear them down—with united effort, we can accomplish lots of things. Involve yourself in full faith, believing that it can be done, and it will be done in no time. This is our mission. This is our call. With hands joined together, we will win—indeed, we won!

## B: MANIFESTED THROUGH TOLERANCE

When people have something against you, all that you do becomes wrong. Just keep doing your best to make things right. No one can please every person in the room. As you come to the middle of the crowd, each person will have their own opinion, judgment, preference, and most of all, prejudices about you. Comments on what you wear, how you carry yourself, how you talk and walk, and how you answer questions will be positive or negative. The people in the right-hand corner might praise you and the people in the opposite corner might criticize you. It is a challenge when you are expected to act according to preconceived ways; when you do not conform, others around you might say things that you might not like to hear.

When you are confident about yourself, there is nothing that can intimidate you nor can others' comments affect the way you look at yourself. You may change here and there, but we cannot live by and through the comments of other people; however, this does not also mean that we are careless enough not to do the right thing. We are to do right, no matter what, and we are to make sure that whatever criticism we receive is welcomed with open arms. It's up to you to evaluate others' comments (especially those who are managers, supervisors, or leaders of your organization), to take a moment to ponder whether their perceptions of you will be negative or positive.

When we allow criticisms to affect the way we think of ourselves, we have a very serious problem. People will speak up, but if we know who we are, then we have nothing to be worried about. Critics may aim to destroy us. But when criticism magnifies a reality in our lives, we'd best accept it and mend our faulty way(s),

We are facing a world where selfish gain is at the forefront of the agenda and where people don't care if they have violated someone else's rights. It is empowering, knowing that you are doing what is right no matter what and regardless of what other people will say. "The steps of a good man are ordered by the Almighty delighted in their ways." We are not people pleasers; rather, we are God pleasers.

People who have a lofty status in life face similar challenges in doing what is right, and they must fight those whose inclination is to harm people and properties because of envy. Be aware that every person has different experiences in life.

When we point to someone else's fault, three fingers are pointing back at us; it is safe to be more cautious and be aware that we are also subject, one way or the other, to the same mistakes. We are made differently, and time shapes each of us in a different manner. We grow differently from each other; some may be slow, and others may be a lot faster.

## C: DOING DAILY TASKS – MANIFESTING EMPOWERMENT

"Be of service. Whether you make yourself available to a friend or co-worker, or you make time every month to do volunteer work, there is nothing that harvests more of a feeling of empowerment than being of service to someone in need." ~ Gillian Anderson, Foreword, *Girl Boss*

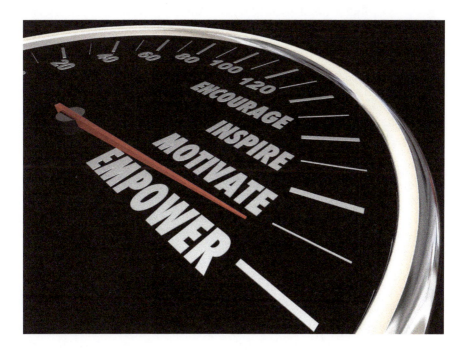

My daughter and I decided we would work together on the daily tasks of preparation, cooking, juicing, and cleaning up, while I undertook the caregiving for my daughter. I had to be hands-on, doing what needed to be done so every detail of the protocol would be properly implemented.

I understand everyone has a different definition of the word "empowerment" and how it relates to us individually. My daughter and I have many differences, but we needed to collaborate in finding a common ground and accomplishing the daily chores that contributed to the process of healing.

By participating either in discussion or implementation, both me and my daughter had to agree upon certain things, opening the door for dialogue and healthy discussion, allowing each other the freedom to speak our individual opinions.

Let's me share, as an example, the success of Google and Zappos. Both companies offer a great deal in staff empowerment. Zappos is even moving to a "flat" organizational structure, where bosses are limited in number.

With empowerment, what you want to achieve is the feeling that every employee has a voice in the company and their input matters. You know an organization has great empowerment when staff talk about "my company" or "our company."

If you look at organizations that have embraced empowerment, you typically see workers providing input on work hours and time management. Plus, you also often see collegial decision-making because these companies really do want to encourage more involvement and commitment from staff.

Me, my son, and my daughter formed a small unit of organization wherein each of us was empowered to share, to open their own ideas on things. Then we evaluated, finding alternatives and different options. I believe this is the reason why my son and daughter are, like myself, always on the management side of retail, leaders in fields we are called to join. I personally have trained them to become managers; at age five, Hannah started on a cash register and my son helped me in merchandising, filling the store with goods.

Yes, the daily tasks we mapped out were done with a continuous consensus on what and how we could improve. We made sure that what we did not only contributed to the greater purpose but was also done in an excellent way.

## D: MANIFESTED THROUGH ASKING THE RIGHT QUESTIONS

Self-talk the person you want to be, not the person you don't want to become. Today, I visited a friend who has been diagnosed with stage 4 pancreatic cancer. She was skinnier than the last time I'd seen her, she hardly spoke, and she was very weak. At any rate, I anointed her with oil of anointing from Pastor Apollo C. Quiboloy, spreading the oil on her abdomen (which was swollen), palms, forehead, legs, and the soles of her feet. As I did so, I was seeking the Father's will for her life, and guiding her in the prayer of repentance, surrendering her will to the Almighty Father, so whether she lived or died, she was of the Lord.

It is not easy to pray for someone whom doctors have already sentenced to death. Her doctor said she might not survive longer than three weeks. It was very alarming, and I pitied her eleven-month-old son, who does not know what is going on.

What we desire is what we invoke in our prayers, it is what we believe in our hearts. Be careful what you ask for because most of the time you will get it the universe will answer our call, will manifest that for which we asked. The Bible says, "Ask, and it shall be given you; seek, and ye shall find; knock, and it shall be opened unto you" (Matthew 7:7 KJV). This is a promise that was made two thousand years ago yet is powerful even now; it makes things happen even in the most impossible situation. The heavenly host, when summoned, responds in a timely manner, granting our wishes. Never stop asking, seeking, and knocking. When we are persistent, an answer will come.

Deep within me, I felt agony in my soul, which wished silently, whispering and begging for help and deliverance. The cry and tears of the righteous are heard even in the farthest planet of the universe. The silent voice of the needy touches the heart of the Almighty, for the prayer of the righteous man is very effective, opening the windows of every opportunity.

Perhaps the most compelling promise of the Almighty is found in these words: "Whatsoever ye ask in my name, that I will do" (John 14:13 KJV). His name is above every name, His name embodies the whole meaning of His coming. There is power in His name, there is healing in His name, and there is deliverance in His name, for in His name we are baptized, soaked, and immersed within the will of the Father Almighty that we may be filled with His fullness.

Today, you may stumble and fall. It may seem everything has crumbled, and you are at the bottom of your resources, at the end of your rope. Yes, He will carry you, comfort you, and provide you a way when it seems there is none. When the doctors say you have three months to live, it sounds terminal. The last call might be sooner than you think, for the truth is we do not know when our life will end. But when the candle is still burning, none of the medical doctors can judge the living.

Those who belong to God cannot be shaken by the fear of death, for whether in life or in death, they belong to the Lord—not by religious fanaticism or denominational affiliation, but rather by an inward transformation in which you open your heart in full surrender to the Almighty Father's will.

Words are powerful. They can create good or evil, can build or destroy. Results depend on the words that we utter. Be careful what we ask for we will be judge to every word we say. We will be judged according to our words as much as we will be judged according to our works.

Before you even say anything, the depths of your heart and your unspoken requests been heard in the heavens. Amazingly, our clear desires and intentions will have answers, and the answers will be for the specific thing for which we have asked. A burning desire fuels and energizes us when we believe, even if what we asked for seems impossible from a scientific point of view, or from a philosophical understanding, or from a theological perspective.

These are the reasons why, when we make our request, it must be clear. Each request must be specific and well-defined, our words explicitly stating what we really want to happen. If our words are ambiguous, our request will not bring about the desire that is in our heart. The clearer we become, the better, for then the host of heaven will find the answer to our request. The heavenly host of angels will understand the request and make your desire a reality. Do you really know what you want? Do you really know what you like? Can you define your purpose? Are you clear in the direction you are going?

Knowing what you like and understanding your wishes will give you greater purpose in the fulfillment of your request. Not knowing what you really want will lead you to a lot of disappointments because when you are not fulfilled, you become dissatisfied and discontent, which eventually leads you to total failure. A lot of people live this kind of life. I feel sad when I see this, because this will lead to depression and death. You must articulate what you want to be, where you want to go, and how you want to make things happen in your life.

I am always surprised when I see people struggling with meeting their goals. The hardest thing, I guess, is awareness: knowing who you are and what you can become, allowing all your energy to flow toward your desires. Is it not true that a person knows, with a mental picture in his soul, "What you can conceive in your mind, you can achieve?" The womb of your dreams is your mind, which has the capacity to think, reason, analyze, understand, conceptualize, and progress, step by step, toward accomplishing gargantuan realities. We have been given the capacity to create and make the impossible possible through the power that lives within us.

# CHAPTER 8

## SUPERCHARGING MY ECONOMY

### A: MANIFESTING RESULTS

It is high time to change our actions, to get excellent results. Each of our actions contributes to the greater purpose we have set our minds to accomplish. Actions create things, build up in an incremental series of little steps that, over time, will build a gigantic edifice. We may have watched building construction, which begins with flat ground and ends with 52-, 85-, or 160-story buildings like the Burg Khalifa, huge and tall buildings that surprise us, rising from the earth in a gradual, steady manner.

As I write this chapter, I am in Hong Kong with my loved ones, looking at the high-rise buildings from the top of Victoria Peak. We are on the viewing side of the Peak tower at the Fuji Yama Mama restaurant. The light-filled, grandiose buildings and glittering surfaces are beautiful, and we gaze out upon them with amazement. The buildings are monumental works of art by those who produce results, regardless of the work involved in preparing, designing, structuring, and building; these magnificent creations are all put together by a unified team. They were brought into being by people who dared not succumb to mediocrity and are excellent showcases of architectural glory.

A lazy hand will never accomplish anything in life, but industrious, hard-working hands accomplish wonderful creations, whether buildings, machines, work of arts, or other masterpieces.

There are actions that make us great; there are also those that sometimes humiliate us. What are the actions that make us great? Why are people reluctant for change? Are we ready to leave our comfort zones? Are we intimidated by things unknown? We experience plateaus because we never dare to try something new, something different from our previously learned way of doing things. We fear making mistakes when we all know we are prone to make wrong choices in many ways.

The decision my daughter and I made to pursue the natural, non-conventional Gerson way was not easy to make. We didn't want to make a wrong decision. The therapy demanded daily organic fruits and vegetables, along with twenty-three different supplements, which we could only order from the USA. The challenge was not where to get these items. There were at least four stores in our area:

If she had made a different decision, had chosen the other way, everything would have been provided free of charge, from chemotherapy to wig supplies (when her hair started to fall out) to support from people who have had the same experience as her. But when it comes to the natural way, even doctors said we were using a quack doctor, not supported by the medical system. We were not supported by the health care system, and there was a feeling that the only remedy the medical system would accept and allow was their own.

From thousands of trials and errors, various experiments, clinical testing, checking results, and evaluating data, Medical doctors claim that chemotherapy is the only way. They claimed to have saved lives for the past seventy-seven years of the system's existence. If I follow this line of thought, that modern conventional medicine has found an excellent way, how many lives have been saved through chemotherapy? And, of equal importance, how many people have trusted in the system and died? This has been a very controversial issue, and those who advocate against it are silenced.

Following the therapy was somewhat pricey, never mind the cost of the regular Skype conferences with her doctor, who coached us in the Gerson way. There were times that we didn't have the budget to keep on; my daughter had already used up her savings and RRSPs. She was even deprived of disability assistance from the government. It was not easy. Nowhere to go except to look up and hope for blessings to come to our aid. They did come, and we were able to make our way every day.

## B: MANIFESTED IN REACHING GOALS

Our purchases of fruits and vegetables were almost two hundred fifty dollars a day, excluding all the supplements and the organic coffee my daughter used for her enema. It was a daily walk of faith, but we persevered and reached our daily goals, which we believed would eventually lead to total and complete healing. We lived one day at a time, not allowing the worries of tomorrow to bother us.

Aiming for the stars is everyone's desire. Since the beginning of time, human beings have aspired to achieve. We are born to win, born to make a difference. We were crafted by the hand of the Divine, individually breathed upon with the life that brought us into existence. We define ourselves according to the master Creator, who provided us with the knowledge to know who we really are. We zero in on the ultimate design, perfecting creation's beautiful manifestation of a perfect man.

Man is created perfectly, designed to accomplish great things in life, and provided with mental faculties that can rationalize and analyze an unlimited amount of information. Man can grasp, understand, assimilate, and create. Man can bring the unseen into reality, providing solutions in perfect harmony with the plan of the Almighty. Yes, human beings can do the impossible. Many creations that had been impossible dreams in the past are today a perfect reality.

Indeed, healing was available not as we wanted it to be nor as we wished it to be, but according to the perfect plan of the Almighty. Where are we heading with these creative ideas and innovations man has brought about for centuries? Are we getting better? Have we really made our world a better place in which to live? Are we really heading the right direction? Answers could vary, depending on the angle from which we see things; our views are sometimes restricted by our vision, which is affected by our belief system and experiences. Our training and education, whether formal or non-formal, contributes to our perceptions. Our views in life are always influenced by our thoughts.

Now man can aim high, achieve what we have not done before—seeing from the perspective of an eagle and with the wisdom of a lion, the power of an elephant, the aggression of a tiger, and the heart of a dove.

We can indeed reach beyond the northern skies, go through millions of galaxies, soaring high above the clouds. I was standing on the ground of the Port of Macau, considering the world's longest sea bridge, which connects Hong Kong and mainland China to Macao. Up in the skies, one of the most significant features I can see is the Great Wall of China, rolling like a twirling dragon as it crosses the land. And when the tallest building, which China is now building, stands, it will signify how humans have achieved their goals and ambitions, unrestricted by gravity. There is no impossibility in anything our mind can conceive, for it can be achieved. There is nothing on this planet now that is not doable, for it can be done, it can be achieved, and it can be created. It *is* possible.

Look at your own personal circumstances and consider the load you are facing. You are perhaps overwhelmed by your own reality. You are stunted, facing the Mount Everest of your own personal difficulties and stressed-out feelings, right? Unable to fulfill your potential, engaging in negativity and paralyzing your capacity to create something good.

When you reach for the stars, you aspire to reach the heavenly skies; looking at their vastness you'll surely be amazed. You will be tongue-tied, for no words can explain the beauty of God's creation, which never ends. Our admiration couples with our endless appreciation. We cannot fathom the goodness and the love of the Creator of the universe. This is because we have never learned to appreciate what we already have. We are always looking for something more. Never satisfied or happy or thankful, we complain and blame ourselves.

Our gratefulness matters, for the universe knows that when we are thankful, we will surely change our situation. Gratefulness changes our status quo from complaining to being thankful for all the good and bad that may come along our way, for both produce in us a great and valuable treasure.

## C: POSITIVITY MANIFESTED

Positivity breeds positivity, much as love produces love, joy begets joy, peace brings peace, and prosperity produces prosperity. When you have a positive spirit, it affects other people, influencing them with your infectious positive attitude. They'll feel good being around you, and they'll love to hang out with you. Why? Because you're a positive influence and make them feel good. Your smile stands out. Your happy and positive demeanor projects life, energy, and power.

Thoughts build on our emotions and create the actions that we take. I remember Stephen Covey's words, "When we start thinking positively, we will reap positive results." When those results are invested, we will create a pile of positive attitude, and when that attitude matures, we will reap good character. Good character creates wealth, and wealth determines our priorities. Our priorities determine our destiny. People with stronger values, when it comes to wealth, give it away. First, they return ten percent back to their church, give ten percent to their favorite charity, keep ten percent for them to enjoy, and put ten percent in savings. The rest they reinvest, whether for charitable work or for spiritual and physical investments. This is truly amazing. The more we sow, the greater the harvest, and when you sow less, the harvest will also be less.

Great results are what make you wake up in a good mood, enthusiastic and excited. That's what kept my daughter and I going as we did the daily routine of juicing and cleansing; every time she had her bloodwork done, we saw better results and improving data. The more we become positive, the more adorable the outcome becomes.

We cannot choose to be pessimists, for it only breeds emotional acidity, creating an ugly picture of our personality. Acidity produces diseases that complicate other diseases until our health becomes worse, leading to cancer. A negative attitude never produces anything good; hate and war eventually end in poverty and death.

If we sow negativity, we reap what is sown. When we sow hate, it creates enemies. When we have lots of enemies, it causes fear in our community, and when fear and hate escalate, it produces war. Never-ending fighting will result in tens of thousands of deaths. A lot of nations are suffering, businesses are closing, families are broken, and lives are wasted, devoid of purpose and direction, because of this. What a sad fate. But we can change the course of our lives by changing our thoughts, actions, habits, and character. When we do that, we will change the world...and we will change our destiny.

That change includes and starts from us, our home, and spreads to our community and our workplaces, when we come to work with excitement, with a smile. Energy builds, and we feel empowered, creating an atmosphere of happiness. This is contagious; it begins with you, then moves to your employees and your customers. The result? High productivity and an increase in revenue. Output is dependent upon input.

Thoughts are critical to your progress or regression. Processes in your brain create action, whether out of love or hate. These thoughts become a person's source of reason and reality, and they will take actions based on their philosophy, which will become an everyday practice—a pattern, a model for that person. Words become actions because of a person's thought patterns.

When these actions are taken repeatedly, they become a habit, a normal disposition, a regular way of doing things. Surprisingly, you don't have to say anything; it naturally comes out. A person doesn't even have to try to do anything he does on a regular basis for it just automatically comes out. Why? Because it's now a habit. When you repeatedly do what you're doing, it will determine your destiny.

Our full awareness of this occurred when the Son of Man came, the anointed, chosen to declare the words of life, the words of the Almighty. None other than our beloved pastor, Pastor Apollo C. Quiboloy, who inherited these words, was the recipient of the fresh manna of revelations and is now the administrator of the Kingdom of Jesus Christ here on earth. He is the king of the new creation. He began declaring the words that brought enlightenment. Our thoughts were awakened, and our way of life has changed. The words have transformed our inner being. Our actions are righteous and holy, and we practice and execute the words, committed only to doing the works of the Almighty Father.

Even the apostle Paul emphasized this, and said,

> **Finally, brethren, whatsoever things are true, whatsoever things are honest, whatsoever things are just, whatsoever things are pure, whatsoever things are lovely, whatsoever**

> *things are of good report; if there be any virtue and if there be any praise, think on these things (Philippians 4:8 KJV).*

These are beautiful words. Our minds must be immersed in these positive thoughts so that we are set to do the will of the Father, our Lord Jesus Christ.

When we are habitually doing only the will of the Father, our disposition is "love, joy, peace longsuffering, gentleness, goodness, faith, meekness, temperance" (Galatians 5:22–23 KJV). All these qualities are manifested daily. We will exhale the positive fruits of the Spirit. Our words are reflected in our lives, making the words alive in us; thereby the words become flesh, become visible, become a lifestyle. Let us walk the talk and talk the walk.

In these last days, the Father Almighty has chosen a man from the fallen Adamic race, who has inherited all things, sonship and kingship and the word of God. Pastor Apollo C. Quiboloy came in a manner that we did not expect. He talked the walk and walked the talk. It is not easy to say, "I am your model" unless the person who says those words knows himself and is confident enough to be an example in all aspects of life; if he wasn't, then the talk could only be talk and would never be seen in the way he walks. But because he lives by what he believes, and what he believes is his way of life, indeed he is worthy of duplication.

This man embodies the qualities of a true spiritual Adam and possesses the spirit of Jesus Christ, who is the second Adam. He walks in all positivity, influencing everyone he meets with that irresistible power, and magnetizing them with the unconditional love of the Almighty. He is a person who knows no limit, exercising faith to the maximum so that everything becomes a possibility. He has unending stories of victory after victory and is triumphant in all his endeavors. He is a legend of faith, conquering every demonic force, overcoming every obstacle. He is not limited to human resources; he is equipped with all the angelic host of heaven at his command. He is the embodiment of loyalty, commitment, and dedication to the Father's will.

No one in this world is like him. He loves the environment, clothing naked mountains in a beautiful majestic display of a wide array of flowers and thousands of pine trees, making the place a scene of heavenly bliss. There is no one who loves nature like him, putting the world's ecosystem back into balance, creating a new world of pristine waters, welcoming angelic visitations. He sees a manifestation of heaven here on earth; one time he said, "You don't have to die to see heaven, for heaven is here." Truly, an encompassing love for planet earth is found in the heart and life of Pastor Apollo C. Quiboloy. Yes, this world would be a better place if every person on this planet could be like him; you cannot imagine what a beautiful world it would be.

## D: MANIFESTING TRUTH

Truth prevails. It cannot be destroyed or ignored, nor can it be denied. The truth remains forever. I remember the saying, "The best way to lie is to say only half of the truth." How can we be liars who claim to tell the truth when we tell only half of the truth? If we do not tell the truth, then we end up telling a lie, even if it is only a lie of omission. Sometimes it hurts to tell the truth, for most of the time, when we tell a lie we fool ourselves. It bothers me when I don't say the truth. It disturbs me when I tell a lie; it bothers my conscience and I have no peace within my soul. The truth, when it's accepted, gives freedom to the oppressed, setting them free of the inward bondage of lies and deceitfulness.

Life would be so rewarding if all humanity shared the same blessing, the blessing of freedom that comes from the truth and nothing but the truth. Lies are the source of fear and deceitfulness and anger. The truth remains the truth, even if no one adheres to it. Truth prevails; it cannot be destroyed or ignored, nor can it be denied. You can't cover up the truth, you cannot change the truth, and you cannot twist the truth. The truth remains, forever. It prevails throughout the course of time.

The medical lies propagated for seventy-seven years, must be expose, chemotherapy is not the only solution that cancer patients have to choose. It's time to tell the truth and live according to the truth. If only the advocates of true, meaningful healing were not silenced, we could save so many lives. I guess there is a higher spiritual influence on those lawmakers, directing them to give approval to what brings higher revenue.

There are different versions of the truth. Some people claim they have the truth, while many say that no one knows the truth. The truth can be found, known, and owned. The truth is immaterial yet can be possessed by truth-seekers. Truth is given in words, receive the word of God, we way one way or the other, has firsthand experience of the truth. When we flip the pages of the sacred writings, we will discover the truth that is freely given to us. What makes these sacred writings confusing is not the content itself; rather, it is that those who handle the content vary in their interpretations.

Truth is words, which feeds the soul in and out, up and down, these words will not fail to manifest the truth of which they speak. The truth is said and done. There is consistency, there is coherence, there is unity, there is understanding, and there is enlightenment. Truth enlightens those with darkened minds, crooked thoughts, and faulty understandings, which come from people who have twisted, changed, obscured, and adulterated the truth.

Today, information is vast and widely available. When you Google something, you'll usually get the answers to your question. Beware, as not all answers are true. The same forces are at war, whether in the written word, spoken word, or audio recordings; two forces are seeking adherents and followers.

# CHAPTER 9

## PRESCRIBING SOLUTIONS!

### A: MANIFESTING INWARD CHANGE

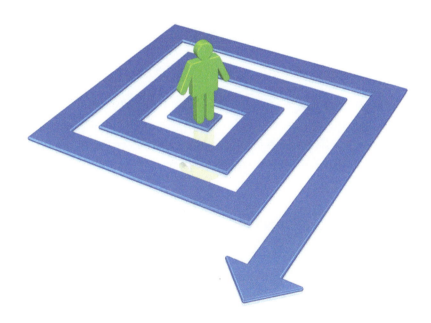

We humans were created in such a way that our inward feelings are always considered by our Creator. For this reason, the science of understanding human behavior was studied and learned, so that through clinical observations and experiments we will have a better understanding of ourselves. We can evaluate why we feel such passion. What motivates us? What weakens us? What makes us stronger? How do we feel in certain situations and circumstances in life? How does good news and bad news affect us? Too many questions to tackle, and so many different ideas to consider.

Deep within us is an unseen reality of what we really are; in every person resides the unseen soul, which has the capacity to think like God, to feel like the Creator, and to make the right choices. These abilities are innate in every human being, and this is real, alive, and will exist forever. That inner person is the real being that really feels. I have been to many viewings of dead loved ones and people; the truth is undeniable—the body is still complete, but there is an absence of feelings, an absence of eyesight though the eyes are still there, of hearing, feeling, seeing, and tasting. Why? Because when the soul is gone, the body becomes dead in the physical world. A physically dead person no longer has a connection to the physical world. That connection is gone, but it does not mean that the person ceases to exist.

As we look at our lives, we go through many different forms of struggle, hardship, difficulty, pain, and distress. Our attitude in dealing with these is crucial: either we become better people, or we become bitter people. It builds us or destroys us, depending on how we respond. What are the things that bother you? What are you facing today that you are greatly emotionally affected by? You must identify these things and face them with courage and determination so that, no matter what is going on in the physical world, you remain steadfast.

Without an inward transformation of thoughts and perspective, we will not be able to change the outer physical part of our being. There must be a change of mind, a change of heart, for the body responds to the mind. The body follows where the mind goes, and it can create the beginning of a new life that emanates from within our hearts. A new heart will I give you—a wider perspective, a deeper meaning of things, and transformation of our innermost being.

This inward change makes you stronger. There is an endowment of spiritual power that comes and lives within you. Whatever happens outside of you does not affect or bother you anymore. If a negative comment you heard still affects you, then you must thoroughly evaluate yourself, investigate yourself, and face the facts without fear. For unless you know who you are and what you are, you cannot be what you have envisioned yourself to be.

## B: *MANIFESTING POWER OF ACTION*

BE EMPOWERED! Make decisions according to sound judgment based on research and evaluation. What would have been easy if you knew how to handle your inner fear and allow your inner strength to dictate your reactions? Do not allow your senses to deceive you about your true feelings. Develop yourself through constant meditative time for reflection. Have a daily plan for reading and contemplating, develop steps of action and procedures, and then make the changes, when necessary, to act on your newly developing systems. Let's act on the message we want to convey, let the words coincide with our actions. We are always expected to do what we say, and when our actions do not correspond to the message we want to say, there will be miscommunication.

For example, a husband and wife have similar struggles in their marriage, and they fail to recognize the value of good communication. They fail to see the true meaning of actions hat may mean a lot to their partner. Failure to see these movements and react accordingly results in major fights and a breakup. It is crucial, in the early stages of any relationship, to know each other well, and to get to an understanding of each other's likes and dislikes, what each wants and doesn't want, to be very observant and cognizant of each other's feelings and aspirations. Two people living together can always expect to have differences; these differences call for greater understanding, patience, and love.

Love is proven during a messy misunderstanding; it is not proven when everything is smooth and lovely, but rather when there are disagreements and conflict. What triggers discussion is that each person has their own understanding of things, and each must accept the other's opinion. If there's no common ground, the blame and pointing of fingers begin. Words of love are important, but what lasts forever are the actions that go with those words. In the absence of loving actions, words of love have no meaning or value. Every action creates memories we can never forget; since memories live forever, let our actions be filled with expressions of genuine love and kindness. True love is seen in action when we love our enemies without any reservation.

Humans are not only emotional, we are also spiritual beings. There is a spiritual realm that each of us enters, many times unknowingly. We must be careful that our feelings will not take us to serious, deep spiritual problems.

For example, if you are still on that emotional plain, then you are still alive within. You must come to terms with reality and realize that unless there is a revolutionary change within you, you will still feel all the negativity of this world. Strength cannot be found anywhere but from the one who created you and me. We must come to terms with

Him; He knows us better than we do ourselves because He created us as unique individuals.

In Hannah's life, we made things happen by putting together our concerted efforts in making Gerson therapy a viable solution. Everything we do has specific reasons that carry possible results if properly executed. Her protocol changes as she progresses. It was an exciting journey that made us live one day at a time.

## C: MANIFESTING OUTWARD CHANGE

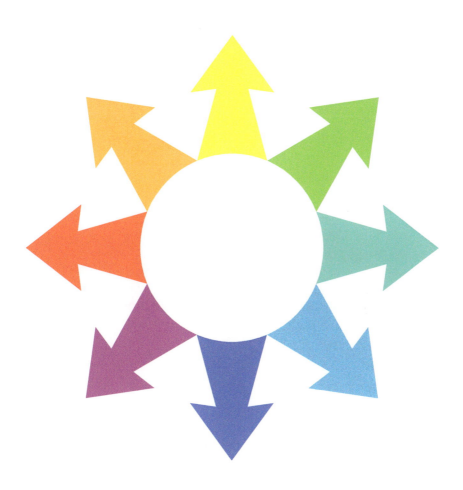

The crucial moment in life is repetitive failure; it is when we keep repeating our mistakes without learning the lessons behind them. When we are aware of our weaknesses, we become more sensitive and cautious so as not to make mistakes again and again. Do you really know who you are? Have you defined your strengths and weaknesses? Begin listing them, accepting them, and start to work on those weaknesses, making them your strengths. Begin by deciding to follow a plan of change.

When you become aware of your weaknesses, then you know how to handle them in a way that does not block your path toward success. Most of the time, what hinders us in doing what is right are the weaknesses we cannot get rid of. We can overcome anything, but the hardest is ourselves. We can only do that when we know how to handle our weaknesses without any difficulty. Mastery of ourselves is very important, for it defines who we really are.

In our weaknesses, He is our strength, as the ancient words say: "I can do all things through Christ who strengthens me" (Philippians 4:13 NKJV). When we are strengthened, we are empowered, refueled with the free energy from on high. The inner person is recharged, soaked, fully bathed in the words that increase courage, life-giving *logos*. The apostle Paul said, "I can do all things." It is you who will do it, no one else; you can make things happen, you can do everything, no exceptions. You've got to believe in yourself, and then unseen forces can move you.

Increase awareness. We perceive things according to the way we see things, the way we understand them, and the way our mental processes download them. We must increase our sensibility to what's valued in eternity: "Lay not up for yourselves treasures upon earth, where moth and rust doth corrupt, and where thieves break through and steal: rather lay up for yourselves treasures in heaven" (Matthew 6:19–20 KJV). Our actions are by-product of our thought processes. Our motivations are the product of our thinking, and thoughts are powerful enough that they can conquer the world or kill your soul. The human mind can do just about anything, whether for the good or bad of the masses.

Increasing awareness includes the following:

1. Being sensitive to your gut and heart feelings
2. Weighing things ahead and evaluating pros and cons
3. Listing every probability, asking "What if?"
4. Listing all possibilities, asking, "What are my options?"
5. Seeking advice; there is safety in having a multitude of counselors
6. Identifying positive and negative impacts
7. Being ready to change
8. Being aware of your surrounding
9. Having a mind that sees things behind and ahead

Know where you are. Don't guess and impress; rather, plan and progress. Know what you want to accomplish, what results you desire. You make your own destiny. You can map your way to success. Use your creative mind to be able to achieve greater understanding of life, better options, and reasonable plans of action. Beware!

## D: MANIFESTED THROUGH ABANDONING THE OLD

Unless you abandon your old, familiar ways, you are not open to a new, advanced way. The call for us to change is a revolutionary call, a call to leave the old ways and embrace a new way, with a new system, a world system whose priorities and emphasis are for the greater benefit of humanity. This new way is devoid of selfish, egoistic desires, and full of a generous and humble way of giving, making sure that wealth is shared with as many as possible, providing for the needs of individuals and families.

We exist so that other people may live, that they may again believe in themselves and rebuild their lives to be a blessing to others in return. As I write these words, I am seated at the food court of Vancouver International Airport, gazing at hundreds of people running to catch their flights, hugging to say goodbye, taking photos for remembrance, with some laughing and telling funny jokes while others shed tears, waving their goodbyes.

Life is wonderful and precious; it's beautiful to live, move, travel, eat, and drink, making the best of this life, creating precious memories. In July 2017, I send off my son to London, the first stop on his series of countries to visit and enjoy while having a fun time with new friends. We had a wonderful time together, chatting about life and discussing the prospects of a beautiful future. He will be away for almost four weeks, leaving behind him the stress of work. A change for a while is an excellent break from the pressures of sales goals, quotas, and training new people.

It's advisable to go for a vacation occasionally, when you can. There could be thousands of reasons why these people at the airport are traveling: work, to visit loved ones, or for pleasure. Regardless of their reasons, they are going, leaving some familiar ways. When they return, they'll take with them the lessons learned on their travels, memories of the new people they've met, and all the wonderful stories they tell.

We must find ways to bring about change; we cannot go around in a circle, always going back to the place where we started, going back to what has been a failure, blaming the past for our present ailments. We have never moved on to see the brighter side of life: the beauty of flowers, and the wonderful songs of the birds that sing in the night. Yes, we must forgive the past, we must forgive ourselves, and we must start again, with a fresh beginning, a renewed spiritual life.

We cannot linger too long in our old familiar ways. We might have thought they provided us with the right path, but instead we ended up circling back to our old familiar ways. We have never moved on. We remain stuck in all our weaknesses instead of being strengthened, enriched, and empowered. We should change our ways, but we cannot do it ourselves. We need a supernatural intervention. The old familiar ways do not provide us life; rather, they make our inner selves sick. The old self drags us to the old path of a selfish, ungodly life, filled with evil desires that lead to evil deeds. We must repent, put to death our old familiar ways so we can awaken in a renewed life of the spirit.

Yes, a new life must emerge from our old familiar ways, a new way to living, a philosophy that changes us from within. This is our renewed life, full of love, peace, joy, and goodness. The old ways are all gone; we have beheld a new way, have been transformed by a new spirit, a spirit that changes our perspective and renews our commitment to truth and justice. Yes, leaving the old familiar ways has begun and will continue until we become the person our Creator wants us to become.

Life is good. We should make the most of it. When we reach the point of no return, we give up all our personal rights, relinquishing all authority to a new governance. We open ourselves to the new horizons of life, greater heights than those we attained previously. A powerful life is waiting for us, whenever we make our decisions in favor of it. We learn from the past, and we move on to a better, progressive future. Learning from our experiences sustains us through tough times; we become much cleverer, much smarter than before. We become wiser, seasoned, and mature, understanding that we can never go back to ignorance and unbelief; rather, we continue the path of knowledge, wisdom, and understanding.

This is what this book has aimed at. It is our humble prayer that we will hit the target with precision and concentrate to what contributes to your personal growth.

# CONCLUSION

How awesome it is to conclude this book while I am at the top of the Sydney Tower, in Australia, on October 26, 2017. Where beautiful scenery down below—buildings in different forms and sizes filled with lights. The light we produce in this darkened world, the brighter the world will become.

Light illuminates our path, allowing us to neither stumble nor fall. It provides clarity, taking away the vagueness of things. It provides heat, while darkness freezes everything. It provides energy, the power that creates technology.

Light comes to us free of charge, for when the sun shines, we are empowered, which mobilizes us to accomplish great things. In the absence of light, we can be led to fear, confusion, and disintegration. The value of light is so important that it cannot be wasted.

Rather than wasting them, we must maximize all resources, take every part beneficial to humanity. When I was a young boy, growing up in timber-producing city, we used a lamp for light. We used an empty bottle, putting a hole in its cover, inserting a gauge, and filling the bottle with kerosene. When lit, it produced light, which partly dissipated the darkness.

I see the dividing effects of light as I fly from Sydney back to Vancouver. Everyone on board notices that when the plane comes near the International Date Line, light can be seen dividing the darkness. In the presence of light, darkness disappears. The abundance of light shines on the whole earth, with a brightness that the human eye cannot see or penetrate.

Today, be thankful for the light and illuminate by doing good, through which evil is overcome. By making use of the resource of light, we can create a better world for ourselves and the generations to come. We are game-changers; while the universe recreates its path, most of us wonder why the climate has changed.

We cannot blame ourselves for these changes, for we cannot reverse the course of time. We are to make amends for our acts today, saving the planet for a better future for ourselves and our offspring. The beautiful view of Sydney's northern border, as my cousin Ruth Maquiling gave me a tour, was fascinating. Surfers enjoyed the white sand beaches and ocean waves. This is a country that takes good care of its environment.

There are steps to take, decisions to make, and if we will not do these things now, tomorrow may be too late. If we brace ourselves now, in collaboration with all the agencies involved, we can change the world. May light illuminate our hearts and help us commit to doing whatever it takes to preserve this beautiful world, for all of us and for the generations to come.

Light also refers to the contribution we make in our community, wherein we provide monetary and/or manpower support certain humanitarian projects which also brings more cooperative *kibbutzim* spirit among people when wealth is shared and not just for some fortunate and blessed few, when real love is expressed not just in words but in deeds, tangibly.

The number twenty-four has often been repeated in the pages of this book. This is a significant age. It represents the wheel of rebirth, a subtle harmony of the earth.

After those long twenty-four months of struggle we finally came into a moment in which we could praise and thank God for everything that we went through. Where he brought us from and the golden lessons we learn in those 17,280 hours, 1,036,800 minutes. Those 720 days were just amazing! In my life, and that of my son and my daughter, light did come, darkness dissipated, and we were illuminated. However short or long our life on this planet will be, it's not about the length but the quality of life we live.

Life that exhibits faith, joy, hope, patience, persistence, perseverance, gratefulness, and love, motivated to focus on the creator and not on the circumstances, has transformed our inner being, and healed our wounds again and again. This indeed is a bright shining light that illuminates our darkened paths.

Illumination begins when light reaches the point that darkness dissipates, and then everything will be filled with light. We may find light at the end of the tunnel and realize that in life there is always hope. I would like to share with you in my next book, "Sentenced to die: To live is a fortune, to die is free of charge" A step-by-step and more detailed medical reports of my daughter's fight against cancer and our struggle with the medical system. I will go through all the details of her story. For the main time, please share the book to as many family and friends you have, they'll surely thank you for that.

# APPENDIX

01. The very last part of the colon, before reaching the rectum, is in an "S" shape and called the sigmoid colon. By the time stool gets to this part of the colon, most nutrients have been absorbed back into the bloodstream. Because the stool contains products of putrefaction at this point, there exists a special circulatory system between the sigmoid colon and the liver. There is a direct communication of veins called the enterohepatic circulation. Have you ever felt sick just before having a bowel movement, when stool material has just moved into the rectum for elimination? As soon as the material is evacuated, you no longer feel sick. This is due of the toxic quality of the material and the enterohepatic circulation coming into play. Because of this, it is important to evacuate when you have the urge. The rectum should usually be empty.

This circulatory system enables toxins to be sent directly to the liver for detoxification, rather than circulating them through the rest of the body and all its vital organs including the brain. This system of veins carries rectal / sigmoid toxins directly to the liver for detoxification.

When a coffee enema is used, the caffeine from the coffee is preferentially absorbed into this system and goes directly to the liver where it becomes a very strong DE toxicant. It causes the liver to produce more bile (which contains processed toxins) and moves bile out toward the small intestine for elimination. This seems to free up the liver to process more incoming toxic materials that have accumulated in the organs, tissues and bloodstream. The coffee does not go into the systemic circulation, unless the enema procedure is done improperly.

*The coffee contains some alkaloids that also stimulate the production of glutathione-S-transferase, an enzyme used by the liver to make the detox pathways run. It is pivotal in the formation of more glutathione, one of the main conjugation chemicals, enabling toxins to be eliminated via bile into the small intestine. So, in other words, a coffee enema speeds up the detoxification process and minimizes the backlog of yet to be detoxified substances.*

*You will need the following materials:*

- *An enema bag or bucket, preferably one of clear plastic that you can see through*
- *A large stainless-steel cooking pot*
- *Organic coffee fully caffeinated, drip grind coffee*
- *A source of uncontaminated water. Chlorinated water should be boiled for 10 minutes.*

*The see-through enema bag/ bucket is preferable, but an old-fashioned type that doubles as a hot water bottle can be used although it is hard to tell how much is used at each pass. Do not use any bag with a strong odor.*

*Procedure*

1. *Put a little over 1 quart of clean water in a pan and bring it to a boil. Add 2 flat tablespoons of coffee (or the coffee amount that has been prescribed for you, the Gerson Program recommends 3 rounded Tbsp.). Let it continue to boil for five minutes, then turn the stove off, leaving the pan on the hot burner.*
2. *Allow it to cool down to a very comfortable, tepid temperature. Test with your finger. It should be the same temperature as a baby's bottle. It's safer to have it too cold than too warm; never use it hot or steaming; body temperature is good.*

3. Next, carry your pan or pot and lay an old towel on the floor (or your bed if you are careful and know you won't spill – for safety, a piece of plastic can be placed under the towel). If you don't use an old towel, you will soon have many old towels since coffee stains permanently. Use another bunch of towels, if you want, as a pillow and bring along some appropriately relaxing literature. Pour the coffee from the pan into the enema bucket without getting the coffee grounds in the cup. You may prefer to use an intermediate container with a pour spout when going from the pan to the enema bucket. Do not use a paper filter to strain the grounds. Put your enema bag in the sink with the catheter clamped closed.

4. Pour the coffee into the enema bag. Loosen the clamp to allow the coffee to run out to the end of the catheter tip and re-clamp the bag when all the air has been removed from the enema tubing.

5. Use a coat hanger to hang the enema bag at least two feet above the floor; on a door knob or towel rack. The bucket can rest on a chair, shelf or be held. Do not hang it high, as on a shower head, because it will be too forceful, and the hose won't reach. It should flow very gently into the rectum and distal sigmoid colon only. It is not a high enema or colonic. Allowing it to go well up into the colon may introduce caffeine into the general circulation as though you had taken it by mouth.

6. Lie down on the floor on your back or right side and gently insert the catheter. If you need lubrication, food grade vegetable oil such as olive oil, a vitamin E capsule, or KY jelly should be fine, unless you are chemically sensitive. It is generally a good idea to avoid petroleum products.

7. Gently insert the tube into the rectum a few inches and then release the clamp and let the first 1/2 of the quart (2 cups maximum) of coffee flow in. Clamp the tubing off as soon as there is the slightest amount of discomfort or fullness. Do not change positions or use an incline board to cause the enema to enter further into the colon; this defeats the purpose of this type of enema.

Try to retain the enema for a minimum of 12 or more minutes. Sometimes there will be an immediate urgency to get rid of it and that is fine. It helps to clean the stool out of the colon so that next time around you can hold more of the enema longer. Never force yourself to retain it if you feel that you can't. When you have clamped the tubing, remove the catheter tip and void when you must. It is best to hold it for at least 12 minutes each time. After you have emptied the bowel, proceed with the remaining 1/2 quart and likewise hold that for at least 12 minutes, if able, then void.

The goal is to have two enemas, not exceeding 1/2 a quart (2 cups) each, that you are able to hold for 12 to 15 minutes each. Usually 2 or 3 times will use up all the enema, but that is not your goal. (The Gerson Program recommends one 4 cup enema) Being able to hold it for 12 to 15 minutes. When you have finished your session, rinse out the bag and hang it up to dry. Periodically run boiling water, peroxide, or other comparable antimicrobial agent through the empty bag to discourage mold growth when not in use.

If you feel wired or hyper or have palpitations or irregular heartbeats after a coffee enema, you should reduce the amount of coffee, usually by half, for a few days or weeks. Or consider that you really need organic coffee. Be sure the source of your water is good clean chemical-free spring, well, or filtered water.

Sometimes you will hear or feel a squirting out and emptying of the gallbladder. This occurs under the right rib cage, or sometimes more closely to the mid line. If after a week of daily enemas, you have never felt or heard the gall bladder release, you should consider making the coffee stronger, going up in 1/2 tablespoon increments per quart, not exceeding 2 tablespoons per cup. Alternately, you may need a slightly larger volume, such as 3 cups at a time. Sometimes, 3 enemas (2 cups or less each) rather than two at a session are more beneficial for some.

Always discontinue the enemas if there is any adverse reaction whatsoever and discuss it with the doctor at your next appointment. If you find the enema helpful, do not use it more than once per day for any extended period without medical supervision. Use it as necessary, perhaps several days in a row, but more commonly a few times a week.

 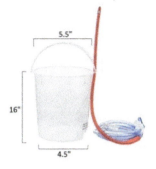

**Positions for using an enema:**

- **Left-side position:** Lie on left side with knee bent, and arms resting comfortably.

- **Knee-chest position:** Kneel, then lower head and chest forward until left side of face is resting on surface with left arm folded comfortably.

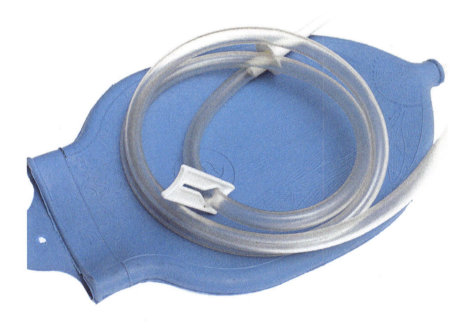

# DINDO GARCIA MAQUILING

Dindo Garcia Maquiling, BSc, is a freelance writer, speaker, and author of countless life-changing messages. He is also the executive director of the Children's Joy Foundation, Canada, and a board member of the Children's Joy Foundation, International Ltd. Having assisted in the creation of shelters and daycare centers and ensuring children are fed, clothed, and sent to school, his passion for resolving the plight of poor, hungry, and destitute children is clear, as is his desire to lead all people to a meaningful and rewarding existence. As a former pastor and ordained minister of Community Baptist Bible Church, he has held various leadership and management positions, through which he has helped countless people live each day to the fullest, creating a legacy of hope, love, and peace. Personally, he has overcome all sorts of hardships and obstacles, including his daughter's victory over cancer. All these experiences have taught him how to live above the difficulties life throws his way, a lesson he endeavors to pass on through his writing and teaching. To learn more about Dindo, please visit https://enjoylife-coaching.ca.

Lightning Source UK Ltd.
Milton Keynes UK
UKHW051018021118
331642UK00009B/150/P